STOP PEEING ON YOUR SHOES:

AVOIDING THE 7 MISTAKES THAT SCREW UP YOUR JOB SEARCH

BY JULIE BAUKE

Published by Julie Bauke

Printed in the United States of America

Julie Bauke
    Stop Peeing On Your Shoes:Avoiding The 7 Mistakes That Screw Up Your Job Search, by Julie Bauke
    ISBN: 1-4392-4650-5

Art work by Mike Ferrin

To the Bauke Boys

John and Matt
Two great teenagers who shouldn't have to endure my cooking,
but bravely pretend it's edible.

Willy, Tito and Jimmy
Three sweet canines who keep my feet warm.

Greg
One wonderful husband who believes in me every day, in every way.

TABLE OF CONTENTS

LET'S JUST CUT TO THE CHASE. WHEN DO I START AND WHAT DAY IS PAYDAY?

GRAB A CUP OF COFFEE AND LET'S TALK.

First, you may wonder, why "Peeing on your Shoes?" Admittedly, it is a bit crude. The title comes from my ten years as a career consultant. I've watched my clients stumble out of the gate in their job searches floundering because of what they didn't know. I used to say to them, "Now let's see how much you've already peed on your shoes." Hey, I know the visual isn't pretty, but you know what I mean, right?

After ten years of working with what seems like a zillion unemployed clients, I think I've seen it all. The crazy stuff, like the client whose interviewer fell asleep in the middle of the interview, the joy of seeing a client land a job better than they had dared to hope for, the heartbreak of seeing three potential job offers disappear in one afternoon, plus a whole bunch of "you'll never believe what happened today…"

It's scary being unemployed. It's a time of great fear, pain, and hope. It's sometimes filled with great happiness. I'm thinking of the client who got the news that she'd been laid off. She sobbed uncontrollably, not because she was upset. She couldn't believe her good fortune. I think her exact words were, "You mean I get to leave this hell hole AND get severance?"

Going through the experience of looking for a job when you don't have one is like nothing you've ever done before. I try to explain to clients what they could expect from themselves, from those around them and from potential employers. Not all of it is pretty. In fact, much of it is downright ugly. It is an emotional rollercoaster unlike any currently in operation at any theme park in the world. On some days, you will feel as if you've bought a season pass to Hell's Amusement Park.

But, there are other days when you will feel like you are not only going to be okay, you are going to be better than ever. In fact, my hope for you is that when your search is over, and you are getting ready to start your new job, you will be overcome with the desire to send a thank you note to your old company. Without them releasing you, you never would have gotten the opportunity to find this new job—one that is even better than your wildest dreams.

Don't laugh. I'd like to have a nickel for every time I had a client say that, in retrospect, they are glad to have been laid off because 1) they didn't realize how miserable they were, or 2) they know that they never would have acted on their own.

I'd have one huge jar of nickels.

This book is the result of me saying one too many times, "If I could spend 15 minutes with a job seeker, I could easily tell them what they were doing wrong. In another 15 minutes, I could tell them how to correct their mistakes." I don't have time to meet with every job seeker. Think of this book as our consultation.

Let's shine a floodlight on your job search and see what's really going on. Be honest with yourself. What can you do differently? What can you do better?

We all deserve to use our gifts fully, and work is one expression of those gifts. Have the courage to dig deep and figure out what is unique about you, or as I like to put it:

What do you "rock at" like no one else?

MISTAKE #1

JUMPING INTO THE FIRE
(WITHOUT YOUR FIREPROOF UNDIES)

BE THIS GUY...

Dan called in a panic. He had just received the word that his job was being eliminated. Being an action-oriented guy, he called me right away. He already had a plan in place. He started to tell me all about what he was getting ready to do. He had compiled a list of contacts, and he was going to begin attacking that list. I was just a name on his list, but at least he had the foresight to start with me.

I stopped him in his tracks when I asked him, "Why was your position eliminated, while your peers are still employed?" He stammered, "I don't know. Maybe because I fell short of my goals this quarter?" He realized quickly that he should not call another contact until he could answer that question, as well as the other questions in this chapter.

...NOT THIS GUY

Matt called me three months into his search. Things weren't going well and he couldn't figure out why. He had networked with dozens of people and was getting nowhere. In fact, most of his conversations didn't even lead to introductions to new networking contacts. I asked him to tell me his story. After listening to him for ten minutes, the issues were obvious. He couldn't even tell me in a coherent way who he was professionally.

No wonder his networking contacts were less than helpful. They had no better idea as to how to help him after talking to him than they did before the conversation. Imagine Matt's dilemma. He now had to craft his messages and try to convince his contacts to give him another chance.

Oops.

When you find out you've lost your job, the temptation to jump into action can be overwhelming. It might be impossible to resist. Regardless of the reason—layoff, plant closing, replacement of the entire leadership team, poor performance—it just doesn't feel good to be told that your services are no longer required.

When I worked as an outplacement consultant, I often contacted new clients to meet with them and help with the job search. Often, I would get some variation of, "Oh, I don't think I need your services. I already have a lot of opportunities," or "I already have a recruiter working for me." (That second one was a big warning sign that they were clueless. Recruiters don't work for you. You are not their client. More on that later in the book) I would cringe when I heard either of these responses. I knew that there were probably a zillion things they were already doing, or were going to do, wrong as they began their search.

And that's what I call "peeing on your shoes."

There are two reasons that we gravitate toward this type of unproductive activity. First, it's human nature that when we are made to feel bad (for instance, when we lose our job), we move toward things that make us feel good. We call all of the people who know us, and will agree that we "most certainly did not deserve to be laid off!" They know as well as we do that the company did not know what it was doing, that they will regret their mistake, and can't survive without us. And on and on and on. "Oh, and by the way," we say, "let me know if you hear of any jobs. Is your company hiring?" That scenario is a mistake on so many levels I don't even know where to start.

The second reason that the newly unemployed jump into the job search too soon is that we confuse action with productivity. Any action is better than no action, right? So we get on the phone, make lots of calls, and proudly tell our spouse that we have applied to 100 jobs online and sent out another 100 resumes, <u>ALL IN ONE WEEK</u>!

All that activity feels so good. Surely, we think, something will hit. After all, look at all the work I've been doing. The truth is, it probably won't help you get a job. That's the "throw it against the wall and hope something sticks" job search method. It's basically useless, and I don't recommend it.

Like all the other parts of our lives, things always go better when we "think, plan, and then act." Unfortunately, what I see most often is "act, pee on shoes, think, plan." The worst part about searching this way is that by the time you realize what you are doing wrong, you have already made mistakes with your key contacts, and they may be very hard to repair.

Before you jump into your search, you should have well thought-out, road-tested answers to basic questions that you are going to hear over and over again.

Why are you out of a job? aka
The Departure Statement

What happened at your old job? Why are you unemployed? Why did you leave? Why you? Did you do something bad? Okay, the last one will never be asked directly. But don't kid yourself, the people you will be talking to are suspicious. Unless everyone in your department or company was let go all at once, the question is lurking. Most people are just too polite to verbalize it.

You have to be ready with an answer that is positive (or at least neutral). Your answer must reassure people, as much as possible, that it was not something you had done. And if it was your performance that led to you being let go, how you answer that question is critical. In this case, <u>HOW</u>

you say something is at least as important as <u>WHAT</u> you say.

"Bitter and angry" do not rank very highly on hiring managers' list of key qualities they look for in their next employee. Your networking contacts will not refer "bitter and angry" people for open positions inside their companies, or to other people in their network. It's okay to <u>feel</u> bitter or be angry. But reserve those conversations and venting exercises for your very closest friends and family. Those feelings are completely normal, but they are certainly not productive. If you feel angry and bitter right after you are let go, avoid discussing your departure until you can at least talk about it without throwing in choice words for your old manager, and/or crying.

Here are some examples of the good and the bad:

Situation: A CFO (Chief Financial Officer) was removed from his job after 10 years with the company when a new CEO was hired. The new CEO wanted to bring in the CFO he had worked with at his former company.

Believe me, this happens all the time. In the senior executive ranks, either it has happened to you, or it has happened to some other executive in your circle. That means the chances are good that the person listening to your departure story is somewhat sympathetic to your circumstances. The way you answer their questions about the situation will either confirm that their sympathy is warranted…or turn them off to your plight. Let's look at the wrong way, and the right way, to answer the "departure question."

Mr. Bitter and Angry: "Last Spring, the Board, in it's infinite wisdom, decided to bring in this guy from outside the industry. He had virtually no knowledge of our products, or our customers. After a few months on the job, he started axing the very people who had built the company. He threw out everybody, including me, who had any clue what was going on. Then he replaced us with his cronies. I tried to talk him out of it, but he was too stubborn to listen. So, after ten years, I was let go."

Mr. Prepared: "Last Spring, our Board brought in a new CEO. After he had been on the job for a few months, he started bringing in people that he had worked with in the past. As you know, that happens a lot in these situations. Over the past several months, he has replaced four out of the top five leaders in the company, including me. Of course, I was disappointed. But I had ten good years at the company. I learned a lot, and I accomplished quite a bit. My experiences there have put me in a position where I can move into the top finance role at a new organization, and contribute immediately."

Put yourself in the shoes of the interviewer and re-read those statements. Which person would you be more likely to hire? You do not want to put the interviewer in the position of deciding whether he should believe you. The interviewer may be sympathetic to your plight. But his goal is not to help you feel better about what happened. For him, it is all about moving forward, NOT about the woes of your past. That is Not. His. Problem. Get your sympathy from your spouse, your close friends, or your dog. Let your interviewers and networking contacts see that you are focused on the future and ready to move on from the past.

Obviously, some situations are much easier to explain. For example, a massive layoff, or a company that closed down completely is very easy to explain. But you need to be ready for the "departure question", no matter what.

True Story! Really!

Mary Pat worked for a major U.S. company that had been on a downward slide for years. She was part of a regional team that, at their heyday, had 300 people on it. She survived six layoffs and ended up being one of the last dozen standing. I think most people would assume from that fact that she was pretty darn good at what she did. But she was prepared with her departure message—and it was a good thing she was.

She encountered an interviewer who would not let go of the fact that there were still 11 people left. This person acted as if she were suspect because "if she was any good, she'd still be there." Huh? I don't get it either. But you have to be prepared for that guy, and then just hope that you don't encounter him.

Your departure statement is a "get past" question. It will be asked early on in the interview. You don't want to blow it, because that may throw you off your game for the rest of the interview. At the very least, if you answer it ineffectively, the interviewer may keep a seed of doubt about you in the back of his mind. You can prevent that with some forethought. Remember, one tiny seed of doubt might be enough for the company to pass you by, and pick the next guy.

What should we know about you? aka TMAY (the dreaded Tell Me About Yourself)

You reach out to people quickly because you want their help, right? Well, how can they help you if you aren't ready to deliver a concise, well thought out answer to this question? Your answer should be 2-3 minutes in length (any more than that, you will see eyes glaze). It should focus on your professional life only. Give them the highlights of what you have done and where you have done it. Do not include the stuff that you never want to do again.

Remember, this is your opportunity to frame your experiences in a way that highlights the best of you. It will drive the next part of the conversation—and where it goes from there. Why only professional stuff? If you use your three minutes talking about your children or your outside activities, you can come across as a less than serious professional. That may be fair or unfair, but that's just the way some people will see it.

I had a colleague once who asked this question with a very clear intent. He wanted to know what, given a few minutes of unstructured "air time," you would choose to talk about. He found the answers to be quite insightful. I would agree. You may be thinking, "How can I get all of my professional life down to three minutes?" It's a great question. Maybe now you can see how important it is to spend some time figuring out your answer to this one before you start picking up the phone or meeting with people.

Ms. Unprepared's answer: "I'm a really hard worker with a lot of experience. I've done a lot of things. I've prepared marketing plans, run trade shows, and created brochures. I did a lot of that for my church too. A few years ago, we had a big conference and I did all of the marketing. I like to do big projects, but I can do small ones too. Like the time I organized an event for my boss. That was fun but a lot of hard work. I think I'm best when I have a good team around me. But I can work well alone too. Oh yeah, I am also a Sunday School teacher. I just love people."

Ms. Prepared's answer: "I am an events planner. I have experience in developing, planning, and executing events that range in size from 100 to 10,000 attendees. I am at my best when I am involved from concept development all the way up to, and through, the day of the event. I am a creative, strategic thinker who is able to assemble a team of skilled professionals that deliver.

In my most recent position with the ACA, we decided at a very late date to hold a regional conference. It was a very challenging event to pull off, especially with our very limited budget. By rallying our team and our outside resources, (and with a few very late nights), we held an event for 3,000 that was our most successful event to date. Members are still asking when we can do it again. I have worked across industries, and enjoy working with member focused organizations. Their events are highly complex, and they require the full range of my skills."

Now ask yourself—after reading these, which one gives you the "visual?" Which one gives you an idea about how to be helpful? Which one inspires confidence that this is a professional that you want to either hire or introduce into your network?

Here's the really important question: which one do you want to be? Do you really think that you can be that person an hour after losing your job? I didn't think so.

True Story! Really!

Pete landed an interview at his dream company, and had been advised several times to prepare thoroughly. (You can't anticipate what will be asked, but you can reasonably expect that you will be asked the TMAY question at least once in your search.) He showed up ready for action. The first question? You guessed it. TMAY. Pete froze, and yes, there was pee landing all over his wingtips. He fumbled his way through something resembling an answer. He knew he had not started well, was now at a disadvantage and he never recovered. You can bet he was prepared the next time, but what a costly lesson!

What kind of job are you looking for?
aka What's next?

That's why you're calling, right? You are looking for help. Even if you are just calling to share the news about what happened, you will surely be asked this question. I believe that people truly want to help, but you have to help them to know how to help you. Answering this question clearly and concisely is absolutely essential, if you want to enlist their help.

Helpful Hint: "As little as possible" is not an acceptable answer to the question, "What kind of work are you looking for?" My response when I hear someone say this? "I'll let you know when I hear of someone looking for someone to do as little as possible." Same goes for answers like, "Sell snow cones on the beach in Hawaii." Even if that is your fondest desire, think of what message that is sending. If you are joking, you still might leave a little doubt in the minds of the people you are talking to.

Let's look at two possible ways you could answer the question:

Mr. Not Ready's answer: "I'm really not picky. I am looking for a job in which I can do a lot of different things. I'm really flexible. I've managed teams and like to improve processes. Really, anything. You guys hiring?"

Mr. Ready's answer: "I'm looking for a position in an organization that is experiencing rapid growth or change and that is looking for someone to drive the process changes and improvements necessary. I am a Six Sigma Black Belt who has a lot of experience in both the manufacturing and logistics industries. In both of my last two jobs, I was in a role where I was responsible for improving a system of processes that were not working well, but were core to the company's success.

I find that I really excel in high pressure, fast moving environments where process change is needed quickly. For instance, I read that the XYZ Company in Nobletown has just acquired the ABC Company and is in consolidation mode. They are working to integrate their two distribution systems as quickly as possible. That would be an example of an ideal opportunity for me."

Who do you believe could help you most effectively? If you were an interviewer, which person would you be more likely to hire? Which one do you want to be?

True Story! Really!

Kristyn was a partner in a law firm, and wanted out desperately. When we first met, she said that she was done with the law. She wanted to make a complete career change, but had no idea what to do next. Knowing that she couldn't begin her search without some idea of what she was looking for, she spent time in the evenings and on the weekends identifying what kinds of jobs appealed to her AND would be a good use of her skills AND would make her happy to show up on Monday morning.

At the end of her soul searching and exploration process, guess what her "new" career was? Attorney. What she discovered along the way was it wasn't what she was doing that she disliked, it was where she was doing it. She is now working in the legal department at a children's hospital, and Monday mornings make her very happy.

Until you are ready to answer those three questions, resist the temptation to act. It is almost guaranteed that you will be asked all three. And if you pick up the phone, or get a face to face meeting with someone, and are unprepared, you will most assuredly come across as unprofessional, impulsive and possibly emotional. After all, you jumped before you were truly ready. It's not a leap to assume that you will approach a new job the same way, is it?

Setting realistic expectations before you start

True Story! Really!

Brad was a Chief Financial Officer in the energy business. He had spent his entire career at one company. On a lark, he applied for another CFO job that sounded like one he would like to have. The problem is that he didn't have two out of the three requirements—he was not a CPA, and had no experience in the healthcare industry. They were clearly stated as "must-haves." Undaunted, he applied anyway.

Would you have applied? I don't doubt that many, many candidates who likewise did not have the three requirements were scared away, with good reason. It was a long shot for Brad, at best. He was surprised to get a call asking him to come in for an interview. The company was intrigued by his background and wanted to meet him, although they warned up front that he did not meet their requirements.

You probably know where this is going. He's been there for three years now. They told him when they made him an offer, that after meeting him, they re-thought their requirements. They realized that they already had a CPA on staff, and that healthcare experience probably wasn't really critical.

Golly. I'm thinking those are "aha moments" they could have had up front with just a teensy bit of forethought, before they jumped into the hiring process.

I tell that story not to encourage you to go apply for everything you are not qualified for, but rather to make this point. Hiring is squishy, wildly subjective, and it often seems to be determined by which way the wind happens to be blowing at that moment in time.

You need to understand that the hiring process is run and controlled by imperfect people. If you expect everything to go smoothly and perfectly, you will find yourself constantly disappointed. Go into your job search with the understanding that things will never go quite the way you plan. It will save you a lot of frustration.

I have had many clients interview for jobs they were qualified for on paper, only to be thanked later for their time with the comment, "We now realize that we are looking for someone with a completely different background than we thought we were seeking." ("Gee, glad I could help....")

Too often, the hiring process seems to work like this:

- Dust off an ad we ran five years ago.
- Throw it out there.
- See who applies.
- Hope we get lucky.

Does any company try something really daring, like actually sitting down with the stakeholders and getting mutual agreement on what the ideal candidate looks like? Or, creating a selection process with well-thought out questions that would get them as close as possible to actually hiring the right person? Or possibly using a thoughtful decision making process? From my experience, anything like this would be the exception.

What do you do about it? That's the hard part. Too often, you won't be aware that a company is using the "I'll know the right candidate when I see him/her" strategy or utilizing the "hiring by gut only" process while you are being put through it.

Human beings are making decisions about human beings—and they are wildly afraid of hiring the wrong person. That's why many companies use (or misuse) assessments. They are looking for a guarantee that they are making exactly the right decision. Unfortunately, those guarantees don't really exist.

All you can do is be aware that this process exists, and vow to look out for yourself. Keep asking questions, and continually align what you can do and have done with what the company says they are seeking. And don't be afraid to say "no thank you" and move on. Having no job can be better than having the wrong job.

While we are on this topic, I know it takes tremendous courage to say no to a real, live job offer when nothing else is on the horizon. Certainly, if it's a matter of putting food on the table, sometimes you have to suck it up. But in that case, never stop looking for something better. You must look out for yourself at all times.

Your company isn't going to find the perfect job for you, nor should they be expected to. The days where companies looked out for their employees are gone. I don't think that was ever a healthy concept or ideal in the first place. It is YOUR career, YOUR life, YOUR responsibility. You can't pay your momma, your career coach, a recruiter, or a job bulletin board to do it for you.

Either he realized the error of his thinking, or was scared of me. Oh well, either way…

Do Sweat the Small Stuff

Remember, you are competing with the general public for jobs. Most of them haven't been smart enough to buy this book. Most people do not know how to conduct a job search. Even people who have miraculously landed several jobs couldn't tell you how they did it. It's just not a skill set we ever developed like we should.

I believe that is one reason why people stay in the wrong job for so long: a really crappy job beats the terror of looking for a new job, which might also be crappy. The devil we know is better than no devil, or even a more devilish devil. (I know, you're thinking I should write really thought-provoking quotes for a living.)

So how can you stand out? In your job search, etiquette matters. How you appear, how you act, how and if you follow up can make the difference. There are a million etiquette books out there on dress and appearance, so I am just going to give you some greatest hits.

Dress and look like you care if you get the job. I'm not talking about high fashion here, folks. I'm talking about effort. Neat and clean from head to toe. Also important: don't overdo the jewelry.

Practice your handshake with someone who will be honest with you. No squishers, and no bone crushers, please.

Don't leave a scent of any kind, as many are allergic or sensitive. I once interviewed someone who I could still smell several hours later. Not the way you want to be remembered.

Look 'em in the eye, and for gawd's sake, SMILE! I'm not talking about a staring contest or a Miss Perky Bubbles act. Just be genuinely interested and curious, even if you decide the job is not for you. They may have another opening that is a perfect fit.

And above all, consider how you are coming across. Put yourself on the other side of the table and in the shoes of the interviewer. Are you presenting as someone they would be proud to call a colleague?

Last thoughts on jumping into the fire

Going into your job search without being prepared is a sure recipe for frustration. One of the reasons I wrote this book was to help you know what you are getting into. When you have an idea what the road ahead looks like, your travel goes quite a bit more smoothly.

You may be a long way from being a Boy Scout, but I'm going to end this chapter by telling you that you need to adopt their motto:

"Be Prepared!"

MISTAKE #2

FORGETTING THAT IT'S ALL ABOUT YOU. (OR AT LEAST, IT STARTS THERE)

BE THIS GUY...

Caroline had a very diverse background and was qualified to do many different things. Over the course of her career, she had managed large commercial properties, run her own business, and worked for a Big 4 consulting firm. You might think that with such range, she would be qualified to do many jobs.

She was definitely capable of performing a variety of jobs. But Caroline was very clear about who she was, what worked for her, and what didn't. Armed with many years of diverse experiences, she had encountered the good and the bad. She was well aware of the things she liked and did very well—and the things she never wanted to do again. She had clarity of purpose, which means she wasn't afraid to tell anyone who she was and what the next step in her career would be. As you might imagine, her networking conversations were fruitful.

...NOT THIS GUY

Janet also possessed a diverse background with a broad range of skills and experience in the field of health care administration. When asked, she could not articulate what value she brought to the table. "I'm a chameleon," she'd proudly say. "I can do anything." When pressed, she'd insist on being vague. Whatever the job was, she could do it—and do it well.

Do you believe that? Neither do I.

Yes, it really is true. It all starts with you. We often say, "It's all about me," with a laugh. We act as if what we want couldn't possibly matter! We'll just leave it to the universe to give us what we should have, right? A job, any ol' job, will do. How many times have you said in a job interview, "I can do anything. I'm a quick learner?"

Whoa! Back up, cowboy/cowgirl!

Let's look at this in a completely different way. What if you could find a job, or a "group of jobs" that allowed you to use most, if not all, of your key skills? What if you had a job doing the stuff you really enjoyed most of the time? I'm not naïve—I know that we all have to do some measure of stuff that we'd rather not. But what if you could minimize the amount of things you don't like to do?

Now let's take another crazy step, and say that this job also allowed you to be in alignment with your values. You could work at something that interested you and—gasp—made you skip to the shower every morning? What kind of life would that be? Imagine! Doing what you love AND what you believe in. (That's right, and I'll throw in a set of kitchen knives, too!)

Before you decide that I'm nuts, at least answer this question: if you really could find that kind of job, WOULDN'T IT BE AWESOME?

I can't fill out your applications, go to your interviews, or physically get the job for you. But I can give you the skills you need to do it on your own. I'm not promising you will get every job you want. But I can promise that you definitely won't get the job of your dreams if you don't at least imagine that it could happen.

So let's start with you. What makes you wildly happy when you work? What is your Perfect 10 Job?

It's important to mentally picture a job that will allow you to be your best, one that will allow you to spend as much time as possible doing the stuff that you are great at. When you picture yourself doing the job you dream of, you increase your chances of getting it. As a matter of fact, visualization is used by professional athletes all the time. A basketball player who mentally rehearses making that perfect basket improves his performance on the court. Visualizing yourself in the perfect job will increase your confidence and ability to get the job you want.

I always ask my clients to describe their Perfect 10 Job, even before they begin their search. This helps them create a benchmark to compare one job opportunity against another. In other words, if you don't know what you actually want, how can you tell the difference between a great job and a mediocre one? Later in this chapter, we will work through some things that will help you determine your Perfect 10 Job. This will give you a standard that you can judge job opportunities against.

True Story! Really!

I had a client who jumped into his search with no planning. This was a very senior level, executive-type guy. He should have known better. He quickly found two jobs that, on the surface, were a fit. He got an offer from each one. He's got the world by the tail, right? He took the one that seemed to be the best opportunity. Nine months later, he was back hunting for a job again.

As we discussed what happened, he realized that one of the jobs he had been offered was a "4" and the other, the one he took, was a "5." In reality, given his skills and interests, neither job was a good fit for him. But without that Perfect 10 benchmark, the 5 looked good. It turns out it only looked good in comparison to the 4.

That's just one example of many. Chances are good that you have a similar story of your own. That's why you really need to think about what job is best for YOU. You can save a lot of frustration and effort if you spend some time planning and contemplating what role fits you *before* you begin your job search.

Don't take the job that offers the best benefits. Don't look for the job with the longest vacations. It's not about the job with the best pay.

The job you want is the one that won't make you want to use that big ol' check to buy a big ol' calendar to mark down the days 'til your retirement.

If you are in the middle of a job search, you probably haven't taken much time thinking about what job best fits you, *and* adds enjoyment to your life. Really, we all deserve a job that gives us the "total package," a job that positions us to be wildly happy and successful. I'm not talking about money, necessarily. (Though money doesn't hurt!)

I'm talking about the feeling that comes from being in your own groove, that spot in which everything falls into place. It's knowing that you are using your most well-developed skills in ways and in areas that add joy and peace to your life. When you find that place, your version of success will follow naturally.

Figuring out what your Perfect 10 Job looks like

Whether you are knee-deep in a job search, or just beginning to look for work, I want you to take the time to go through the quick questions and exercises that follow. It is well worth your time. You are well worth your time. I promise, you'll be so glad you did.

Okay, now let's break it down.

Think about times when you were happy at work. Even if it was just one day, or a few hours. What happened that day? What were you working on? What did you get to avoid? What type of people were you working with? What type of people did you get to avoid? Think of as many of those times as possible. Jot down your answers, and get ready to do some more soul searching. Keep this list of things you loved and things you sidestepped handy as we move through the next sections.

Skills

The great thing about skills is that we all have them. Sometimes we just don't realize that those weird little things we're good at are actually skills. We also have things that we are not so great at—those are areas where we have very few or undeveloped skills.

Don't feel bad about those areas. In an ideal world, I would be able to use a paperclip, a napkin, and a feather to outrival Martha Stewart and MacGyver. But since I would still be sitting there with just a paperclip, a napkin, and a feather, I leave those skills to them. I just move on to what I am good at.

Remember, we can't all be great at everything. We surely can't outdo Martha or Mac. So let's take a few moments to think about what your skills actually are—and aren't.

Strengths

What do you do well? What are your strengths? Your strengths typically come from your knowledge, aptitudes, and interests. The more you know about a job, care about a job, and excel at a job, the better you will do at the job. And if you're going to do well at the job, the best place to start is by actually getting the job.

Think about the skills that might make you a perfect fit for a job. Do you know everything there is to know about the stock market? Do you bake a mean lasagna? Are you great with children? Do you love being surrounded by people? Take everything into consideration. How do you feel about paperwork?

Weaknesses

Now that you've thought about what you do well, take a moment to think about what you are not so good at. Don't be like Janet, my example from the beginning of the chapter. You might have a lot of skills, but you can't be good at everything. No one is.

Think about that. Ask yourself what you hate, and what hates you. If you're not good at managing detail, don't pretend that you are! If the idea of being near elderly people makes you want to grow old quickly and die, don't look for that kind of job! Stay away from that stuff as much as you can.

Remember, the point of your job search is not only to get a job. It's to get a job that you like and are good at. Keep that in mind as you move on to the next section. We're about to delve a bit deeper into what makes you who you are, and what would make the job perfect for you.

And again, it's all about finding the Perfect 10 Job. Otherwise, you'll end up starting the job search all over again when a job you hate makes you go wacky!

Qualities

Just as important as your strengths and weaknesses are the qualities you look for in your job and in your life. What sorts of things interest you? What type of values do you possess?

We're going to examine those two questions in the following sections— and you might be quite surprised when you really start to think about what these things have to do with you and your job search.

Interests

At first glance, this category might seem awfully similar to your strengths. But just because you're good at something doesn't mean you like it.

For instance, let's take a look at Mike. He happened to be really great at influencing people. Some of his strengths were logic, articulation, and the uncanny ability to make speculation look like fact. The result? Mike was a phenomenal lawyer. The problem? Mike dreaded going to work every morning. The money was great. People respected him. But he simply hated his job.

He once told me he would be happier running a farm. Financially speaking, it might not have been the most lucrative choice. But in the grand scheme of Mike's life, being a farmer would have made him happy. There's a lesson to be learned in Mike's story: you can't put a price on happiness.

Of course, not all of us can be (or want to be) lawyers. Sometimes it's hard enough to find a small cubby to call our own, let alone a farm. The point is, our strengths don't necessarily reflect our interests. We need to think about what we actually like.

Take a minute to think about your interests and the things you love. What really makes you happy? Is it animals? The outdoors? Food? Bossing people around? Working with others? The crisp feel of new money?

Think of all your interests, no matter how irrelevant they may seem, and incorporate those into your list. You may not be able to land a job that utilizes ALL of your interests. But if you can squeeze at least a few of them in there, you'll be much happier at your new job than most people are.

True Story! Really!

Leslie loved art, and anything having to do with art. She spent her free time with artists, and loved watching their projects come to fruition. She spent many weekends traveling to and exploring museums and galleries. Leslie had not an artistic bone in her art-loving body. In fact, she worked at an accounting firm!

When she lost her job, she decided to seek out an opportunity to align her life with her interests. She focused her search on organizations whose mission was related in some way to, you guessed it, art. Her passion was totally evident in the interviewing process. The organization she eventually joined knew that she would be a great hire, and made her an offer despite the fact she had spent her career in accounting firms. As she said, "I have the best of all worlds. I actually get to walk past new exhibits on the way to my desk. How great is that!"

Values

Your values are just as important as your interests. Everyone has a set of core beliefs. You should never have a job that goes against what you believe in. If you wind up with a job that tears at your very soul, you won't really be able to enjoy yourself, no matter how much money, job stability, or potential for growth there might be.

So now take some time to think about the values that are really important to you. Do you believe in the sanctity of marriage? If so, you probably shouldn't search for a job at a divorce court. Do you believe that animals should be seated *at* the dinner table rather than *on* it? Then you probably shouldn't get a job in a steakhouse. Do you believe in an honest government? If you do, you should probably stay far away from politics. Just kidding. Sort of.

The point here is that we all have values and we should be able to stick to them in an ideal job. Even if it means you don't find a Perfect 10 Job—or even a Fantastic 9 or a Super 8—you should never do anything that goes against your values. Make sure you know what those values are before your Perfect 10 rapidly transforms into a Mediocre 5 or a Blah 2.

True Story! Really!

Wayne took a job at a large financial services firm. The economy wasn't good, and he settled for the job out of necessity. He knew he was settling and was unhappy from day one. This particular firm had a company-wide screen saver that resided on every desktop. It said, "What did you sell today?" Wayne said that every morning, he would answer the question to himself as it popped up on his screen: "What did I sell? My soul." As soon as the economy turned around, he was outta there.

Soul Searching

You've gone over your strengths, weaknesses, interests, and values. Now it's time to take the knowledge that you've gained about yourself, and apply it to your job search. In this section, I've provided you with some open-ended statements about what you'd like your next job to look like. I've also provided some examples of ways that you might finish each statement. Finish these statements with ideas that apply to your own life.

Hey, I might be a coach, but I'm not psychic! Only you know the best ways to fill in these blanks, so hop to!

In my next job, I'd like to spend more time …

…working directly with customers.

…planning projects.

…taking on a leadership role.

…being alone than with coworkers.

In my next job, I'd like to spend less time …

…managing people.

…traveling.

…talking on the phone.

…attending company meetings.

I never want to _____ again.

…work with food …

…go anywhere near a retail setting …

…touch large amounts of data …

…handle angry customers …

I am known among my former colleagues to do a great job …

…planning fabulous events.

…handling multiple assignments.

…calmly handling insane clients.

…staying organized.

But, my former colleagues never came to me to …

...handle great amounts of detail.

...fill in for them.

...help them meet a deadline.

...handle sensitive employee situations.

My ideal job type would be working …

...inside a traditional company.

...for myself.

...in a partnership.

...for a small company.

My ideal working hours would be …

...at least 40 hours per week.

...on weekends.

...completely flexible.

...Monday through Friday, 9-5.

I would want to work in …

...a traditional office.

...my own home.

...on the road.

...an office and at home.

I would be willing to travel …

...as much as possible.

...if I absolutely had to.

…once in a while.

…within a reasonable distance.

I would want to work with people who are …

…professionals.

…entrepreneurs.

…creative.

…nowhere near me.

My ideal job would be in a _____ industry.

…Non-profit …

…Governmental …

…Educational …

…Service …

I would want to spend my work day …

Hey, you're on your own with this one! Think of what you would want to do all day; what kind of responsibilities and tasks you would want. More importantly, think of all the other elements you came up with during your soul-searching. THAT'S what you should do with your work day!

Now What?

Any time I get the question, "What are the best jobs now?" Or, "What do you think I should do," my warning system goes off. This person is responding to what the market wants instead of what they want. I am not saying you should ignore the market. If you are the best typewriter repairman in the world, that isn't going to get you anywhere. Nurses will be in demand for a very long time. But I promise you, you would not want me for your nurse. (Remember Nurse Ratched?)

The time you take to consider who you are, where you've been, and what you've learned about yourself is time well spent. For some reason, many of us are afraid to admit that we are not good at everything. If you take a job that is not a good fit for you, or is not the best place for you, you are setting yourself up to be less than successful. At the very least, you will be less productive, and less effective, than you should be. You may even find yourself at the top of your new company's layoff list, and back looking for a job sooner than you expect.

It all starts here. When you get to the point that you can describe the kind of job that would make you happiest, you have a better chance of getting that job, or one close to it. If you know what your 10 is, then you will be able to recognize a 3, as a 3. You will know that you are better off not settling.

Here's a great exercise for you: write a description of yourself, based on what you've learned about who you are and what you like and value. Then let several of your closest professional contacts read it. See if they think what you described sounds like you—the best possible you.

Now you have your map. Start thinking about who you can share it with so that those people can be eyes and ears on your behalf. Don't be afraid to reach for your "ideal." There are people out there who truly do skip across the floor to the shower on Monday morning, instead of experiencing the Sunday night dread that goes along with being in the wrong job.

A little skipping sounds good, doesn't it?

MISTAKE #3

NOT MANAGING BETWEEN YOUR EARS

BE THIS GUY...

Ken was going through hard times at home, and now faced a job search. The economy was tough, and his severance package was tiny, especially compared to his bills. He had every reason to be worried. During the first few weeks of his search, he had a hard time getting out of bed. In his mind, he kept revisiting the company's decision to let him go. He could feel his blood pressure rise as he relived the experience of being shown the door.

Pretty quickly, he realized that was not the sort of thinking that would result in him landing his next job. He began the process of "managing between his ears," as he called it. "It's the hardest part," he said after his search was over, "but I didn't like the guy I was becoming—and I knew no employer was looking for that guy, either."

...NOT THIS GUY

Christine was abruptly dismissed. No warning, no explanation. A difficult situation to be sure. Two months into our work together, she still said at least once during every meeting, "I still don't understand why I was let go." She would tell me that she kept calling people from the company trying to "get answers." Despite my advice—and pleading—for her to find a way to move on, she kept it up. As you might imagine, that train was going no place good. It took her six months to be in a place where she could even speak of her former employer without launching in to a tirade.

Yep. Getting let go is a real kick in the seat. It doesn't matter why, it doesn't matter who else was let go, it doesn't matter what the explanation was. It sucks. The experience often taps into every insecurity we've ever had, as well as creating new ones. But the importance of managing your emotions cannot be overstated. Put yourself on the other side of the interviewing desk. Would you want to hire someone who is still fuming over what happened at his last job?

If you acknowledge that it is at least possible that there are some career transition "almost universal" truths, you won't be so surprised when they happen to you. Some of these truths involve things you need to learn about. Others are experiences you are likely to have while you are searching. Some of them are good things, others, not so much.

Yes, we all think that our doorbell will be ringing with a parade of employers ready to hand us a wildly lucrative job offer. ("A company jet?" you say, "I couldn't possibly... oh okay") We all believe that if we just hang out on the job bulletin boards long enough, we will be discovered as the phenomenal talent we are.

The reality is that if you want to be successful on your job search, you must come to grips with some of these universal truths. Ignoring them won't make them go away. Learning about them before you start searching for a job will make your search <u>much</u> easier. Let's look at some of the truths you need to acknowledge, and what they mean to you.

The Good (yes, there is Good!)

You will learn more about the job market than you knew before. Through your search, you will find out what companies exist, what they do, and how you might be a fit there, today or in the future. You will be well-versed on the economic climate of your community.

You will learn a lot about yourself professionally and personally. You may detest talking about yourself. (Most people do.) But when you are forced into situations where you have to do it, it causes you to have a lot more self-clarity than you have ever had. You will actually get good at talking about your skills, your interests, your accomplishments and your goals. What's not great about that?

You will learn how to conduct an effective search. You will stumble, you will say the wrong things, and you will hit dead ends. Sometimes, you will be absolutely brilliant! If you are like many career transitioners I know, once you get it, you will be able to help others who don't. Other people will turn to you for guidance: unemployed friends, relatives, your kids. (As if our kids will actually listen! I can dream, can't I?)

You should have time to catch up on things you have been neglecting. Regardless of what you may think or have heard, a job search is not a full time job. Not in the sense that you will, or should, spend the amount of time on it that you spent working at your last job. If you're like most professionals, you spent 45-55 hours per week working. If you try to do that in your search, I promise, you will burn out big time. And burned out is not a desirable quality in a potential employee.

You should be spending no more than 28-35 hours per week on your job search. What matters, though, is HOW you are spending your time. By the end of this book, you should have a better idea of where you should be spending your time.

The Bad & the Ugly

It will take longer than you think it will. This is one of the questions people ask me most often. Honestly, there is no hard and fast rule as to how long it will take. People used to talk about the old "six months for every $10,000 in salary" rule, but that doesn't apply anymore. The real answer is a big, fat "it depends." It depends on:

- ⊙ how you spend your time,
- ⊙ how focused you are,

- how clear your messages are,
- what the demand is in the market for your skills,
- how well you interview,
- what the state of the economy is,

...and many other factors.

If you are a nurse almost anywhere, you are likely to land a job very quickly. With other professions, it may take longer. Good ol' Econ 101 applies here: if there is a great demand for your skills, that will undoubtedly shorten your search. If, at the time you are looking, there are lots of people on the market whose skills are similar to yours, your search will probably take longer.

If you spend all of your time glued to your computer, it will probably lengthen your search. However, if you spend your time with appropriate networking, delivering your messages clearly, following up appropriately, and interviewing well, it will obviously lead to a better outcome, in a shorter timeframe.

If you are fortunate enough to get a nice severance package (six months or more), you might be tempted to take it easy for three months, then start the search. Not so fast, hot shot! If your goal is to be employed at the end of the severance period, you may want to get started right away. On the other hand, if you have all the time (and money) in the world, I always recommend taking time off for self-reflection.

Some of the people you believe are your best contacts will disappoint you, and some people you don't know well, will delight you. Yep. It's true. You begin your search with a list of great networking contacts—people who love you, people you are certain will move heaven and earth to help you. You picture the coffee you will share, pouring over his list of key contacts. You picture him picking up the phone and making calls for you, virtually ensuring an entry into the inner sanctums of plush executive suites all over town.

Uh, no.

Our best contacts are "best" for different reasons. Some will provide the great moral support and encouragement that we really need some days. Others will make calls on our behalf. Still others will help us think creatively about ourselves and our searches, or give us a kick in the seat of the pants when it's needed.

Unfortunately, some of your contacts will not be willing or able to help you in the way you'd like them to. Let's say you have a friend who knows every CEO in town. Although it would be nice, I do not think it is realistic to expect her introduce you to all of them.

On the other side of the coin, you will meet new people during your search. You will reconnect with people you don't know well, or haven't spoken to in a long time. Some of them will go out of their way to help you, to refer you to others, and to support you. You will be touched by how some people really step up to the plate on your behalf.

I have always found that the most helpful people are often those who have themselves been through what you are experiencing. Those who have been in the same place for their entire careers may not understand the importance of networking. They may not really know how to help. But don't confuse this with not wanting to help, or not caring about you. You may just need to find ways for them to help that they see as comfortable and doable.

Rejection is part of the game. A really yucky part, but a part nonetheless. You won't get a call-back or an offer every time you interview. Nor should you want one. You aren't a fit for every opportunity that comes your way, and not every potential employer is a fit for you. As much as you'd like to have so many professional suitors that you have to fight them off, it probably isn't gonna happen.

This is not just a process of self-discovery. It is also a discovery of the career market, and all the possible professional opportunities that may be on your radar screen. They will not all be right. If you try to take advantage of every opportunity that comes along, you'll end up being the square peg, trying to fit into the round hole. You will be miserable, I promise.

To find that right thing, you must kiss frogs. Employers kiss a lot of frogs in their search for the right hires, too. Yes, you will be that frog sometimes. It's normal, it's expected, and it's just a part of the journey. The trick to getting through it goes back to that managing between your ears stuff.

You can't let your highs get too high ("I nailed that interview! I can stop my search and wait for my phone to ring! Woooo!"). Your lows shouldn't be too low ("No one will ever hire me. I am going to live in a cardboard box and eat leaves"). Every no is one step closer to a yes.

True Story! Really!

Mary Ann was on top of the world. Her search got off to a fast start- one of the fastest I had ever seen. As you might imagine, I was having little success getting her to slow down and be strategic about her search. Within two weeks, she had three opportunities that were ready to go to the reference checking stage. Then, nothing. She tried to follow up and met with silence. All three opportunities disappeared as quickly as they had appeared. After she picked herself up off of the emotional floor, and was able to move forward, she landed the right job within two months. In our last discussion, she was able to look at the experience in her rearview mirror and reflect. She realized that as difficult as it had been to lose three seemingly great opportunities, the job she took was significantly better than the three that got away.

You may experience changes in your relationships. I have heard it a million times. "My wife/ husband is having a harder time with my job loss than I am!" You think you feel out of control through this process? Think about how the people close to you feel. It is not uncommon for your spouse to be experiencing every emotion that you are—maybe even more strongly!

Spouses, significant others and family members are not only experiencing their own emotions, but they see their loved ones in pain, and experience the pain again. They are angry at the employer, worried about the future, and wondering if their spouse really did something to bring it on, often all in the same 15 minutes. Add to that, the fact that they feel like they can't control or help the situation.

It is very important to communicate not only what you are feeling with your key others, but what is going on with your search. Explain what you are doing and why. Talk about all the important decisions you need to make together, like finances, whether relocation or commuting is an option, and how you tell your children and the rest of your family.

Remember, different generations see work differently. They are likely to respond to your news through their own filters. One client's 90 year-old father couldn't quite believe that he was let go as a part of the elimination of a whole department. He kept searching for a reason he could understand. He actually asked his son if he was "pinching secretaries." We got a good laugh out of that. (Although in retrospect, maybe he knew something I didn't!)

As a result of these job-search truths, there are some things you need to do to be successful. Let's look at a few of those things.

Your Must-Dos

Surround yourself with positive people. Many people will want to tell you about George down the street who has been unemployed for two years, or how bad the market is (even in good economic times). Ignore those people.

Later in the book, we will talk more about networking events. For the purposes of this chapter, let it suffice to say that large groups of unemployed people are filled with negativity and gloom. If you get something out of them, while not being infected by the doom and gloom virus, more power to you.

Remember, you aren't looking for a job for every unemployed person. You only need to land one job to be successful, and you can do that in any job market.

Plan your weeks. Human beings love some measure of predictability and structure—some more than others. When your schedule is torn apart after a job loss, it can really rock your world. Even if you hate your job, it is comforting that there is a place that will actually let you in the door on Monday morning. We know the best route to get there, the best places for lunch, and we know what to do when we sit down. We like the routine, even when we hate the job itself.

Well, say goodbye to structure and predictability. Clients have told me that, especially in the first weeks of their searches, they wake up on Monday, blink, and it's Wednesday—and they are still in their jammies!

Clearly, that won't do. You need a schedule you can stick to. Ask yourself: are you better in the morning or afternoon? Remember, you will and should have extra time compared to your previous work schedule. Should you take every Friday off? Figure out what works for you and stick to it. You are likely to feel bad about taking time off from searching. It's important to keep the guilt tucked away when you are taking much needed time away from your search.

Create accountability partners. It is very hard to do this alone. One of the best strategies I have seen is to pair up with someone who is going through the same process that you are and hold each other accountable. Meet weekly to set goals, share your ups and downs, and keep each other motivated.

Allow yourself time to clean out the attic—mentally & physically. It can take time to really get your mind around your new reality. Beginning a search before you have completed that process can be disastrous. If you have the luxury, take the time you need to "get okay" with your situation and get focused on the future.

Some good old fashioned physical work can help. Create a list of projects that you haven't had time to get to and start making some progress on them. It really does clear your head and allow you to do some good thinking about your "career past" and your "career future."

Look at your financial situation. Get realistic about your finances so you can be realistic about your search. It may not be as bad as you think, or it might be worse. When you know where you stand, it allows you to see your options more clearly.

Take the high road. Always. I know. It is so tempting to let 'em know what you think as you exit. And to tell anyone else who will listen about how you were done wrong. Resist it with all of your might!

True Story! Really!

Ethan was livid about the way his departure had been handled. Sure, he understood that the company was in serious financial trouble. He had even seen it coming and had started packing his personal items. But when his longtime manager gave him the news, he didn't even look Ethan in the eye, or wish him well. And when the company security guard showed up to escort him back to his desk? Well, that was the final straw.

He told everyone who would listen how shabbily he had been treated. He was having coffee with a friend one morning and was giving him the whole story, sparing no venom. Little did he know that seated at the next table, was the brother of his former company's HR Director, who promptly called and told his brother what was being said. Ethan got a call that afternoon from the company's legal counsel reminding him that he had signed an agreement saying that he would not disparage the company—at the risk of losing his severance package.

It took some fancy dancing to get out of that one, but fortunately, he did.

It might feel good temporarily, but I want you to take the long view of your career. How will that make you look? People talk. What do you want them to say about you? "Boy, Sean sure went out in a blaze of glory! Yikes!" Try getting your calls returned if people think all you are going to do is rail on or complain about your former employer. Those are calls (and people) everyone avoids. Besides, you are going to want some of those people to be your networking contacts. (Remember Mr. Bitter and Angry from Mistake #1? He's going nowhere fast.)

Get your skills up to date. Are you ready to compete in today's market? Maybe you need to brush up on your technology skills, or you need to update your knowledge of best practices in your profession or industry. Use this time off to hone those skills. Would you hire someone who doesn't take his own professional development seriously? I didn't think so.

If you are offered outplacement, take it. It's especially helpful if you have never looked for a job while unemployed. Career transition/finding a job is a skill that is never taught—not in high school, college, or by our employers. One of the biggest challenges lies in getting people to understand that they lack job search skills. It is not something you can hire someone to do for you, nor is it something that you can "wing" effectively. The good news is that once you understand how to search for a job, you have that knowledge for life. Outplacement can be one of the best places to learn those skills.

Baseball great Yogi Berra described how to succeed in his sport by saying, "Baseball is 90 percent mental. The other half is physical." While his math skills may have been lacking, his idea is dead-on: a huge part of being successful in anything we do is how we approach it mentally. When you learn to manage "between your ears," your job search will go much more smoothly. Promise.

MISTAKE #4

FALLING INTO THE BIG BLACK HOLE (THE INTERNET, RECRUITERS, AND BAD FOLLOW-UP)

HIT **SEND** AND WATCH THE OFFERS ROLL IN.

BE THIS GUY...

Steve knew the odds and he acted accordingly. He knew that employers hire people, not paper, so his best bet was getting in front of the people who would eventually hire him. But he also knew that technology had a role in his search, so he incorporated the best use of the internet into his activities. He set alerts for the types of jobs he was seeking, then spent, at most, another 3-4 hours a week looking for opportunities his alerts may have missed.

Of course, he knew that the internet was invaluable as a tool for researching people and companies.

...NOT THIS GUY

Stacey started her day online, ended it online, and sometimes spent most hours in between there as well. Even though she knew she was supposed to be networking, she couldn't imagine that conversations over coffee could be nearly as productive as applying to "real, live jobs."

Lots and lots of them.

Tempting thought, isn't it? Rather seductive, really. The promise of online job bulletin boards that bring real live jobs RIGHT TO YOUR HOME! Applying for perhaps hundreds of jobs IN YOUR BUNNY SLIPPERS! And if you believe some of the TV commercials for the online sites, all you have to do is point and click and wait for your yacht to come in.

Nope.

Of course, technology and the ability to actually see thousands of jobs in your home (and in your bunny slippers) is nothing but a good thing.

The problem is how it's used, or over-used, by job seekers. Different studies come up with different numbers, but no matter whose statistics you examine, a very small percentage of people actually get jobs that way. So is that where you want to be spending the majority of your time? I think you know the answer.

Keep in mind also that while those jobs are streaming into your home, they are streaming into zillions of other homes also. Many people less qualified, or not qualified at all, are pointing and clicking on these jobs. They muck up the pool of qualified applicants, making it even less likely that you, the oh-so-qualified one, will ever even be considered. It's almost too easy to apply for any ol' job. Thousands do apply for every job, hoping that if they throw enough online applications against the wall, there will be some that stick.

The pull to hang out online comes from many places. When we are hurting, we're not exactly eager to seek out opportunities for rejection. But your friendly computer never rejects you. It's a safe harbor. Best of all, it makes us feel really productive! "Honey, I applied to 50 (100? 200?) jobs online this week!" Wow. Certainly, someone, somewhere, will recognize your fabulousness!

Maybe not.

Let's break it down. Companies get anywhere from hundreds, to thousands, of resumes in response to online postings. (Yes, the delight of applying online at home with a steaming cup o' joe while watching American Idol wanes when you think about all of the zillions of others who are doing exactly the same thing!)

Imagine the person on the other end of your submission. Just for fun, let's say that she receives 300 responses for the job you are applying for. Chances are, she is also responsible for filling more jobs than just the one you applied for. So let's say she has five jobs to fill. (The real number is probably much higher than that, as everyone is doing more with less.) These are pretty conservative numbers, but even at these numbers, you're looking at 1500 resumes that this beleaguered recruiter has to sort through. Pretty daunting, isn't it?

How do you possibly stand out? Answer: you don't. A recruiter I know told me that he posted a position and got 800 responses. He was faced with the challenge of trying to find even one minute to spend on each resume. Do the math—that is over 13 hours of looking at resumes for one job! That doesn't even include potty breaks!

Let's be realistic. That isn't gonna happen. And even if it did, that's 60 paltry seconds devoted to the resume you worked so hard on. (How did he handle it? I'll tell you in just a few paragraphs!)

Other recruiters and HR department screeners that I have asked about this challenge have said things like, "We got several hundred so I looked at every third one." This was my favorite, "I looked at the first fifty (or the last fifty) and deleted the rest." Yikes.

This is not to say that recruiters or HR professionals are not doing their jobs. They are doing the best job they can, considering the sheer magnitude of responses that technology allows to come to their online doorstoop. And yes, there are some that will spend the time to thoroughly read every single resume that crosses their desk. But I wouldn't bank my future on the odds of that happening.

An undeniable truth in the job search process is that we increase our chances of getting hired when people can see us and experience us in person. That's what we're going for—the opportunity to look someone in the eye and tell our story.

Don't misunderstand me. I am not discouraging you from applying online. Sometimes, the ad is blind (you don't know what company it is), so that is your only option. But, when you do know who the company is, I suggest applying online as a first step only. View it as simply an opportunity to get your resume in the company's system. In my experience, most people do stop there. They believe they are a fit and simply rely on the receiver to connect those dots as well.

You need to be smarter than that. Apply online, then get busy. Find someone in your network who knows someone at the company. Gather info online and in other sources as to what the company's "pain" is. By "pain," I mean the obstacles they face. Every company has current challenges, competitive issues, etc., that they are dealing with. Think about how you may be a fit given their challenges. Why would the company hire you over the other several hundred who applied? If you can't form an articulate, compelling answer to that question, don't expect the company to figure it out for you.

I call this "jumping to the top of the pile." Do you really think that HR person wants to go through several hundred resumes? What if they could find the right candidate without having to do that? That is why networking is so much more powerful.

There are a zillion bulletin boards and job search sites. Get your resume on as many that seem appropriate, given your industry, experience, goals and geography. Set up alerts for the types of jobs you are seeking. Some clients set aside a few hours once a week to surf, then they let the alerts do the rest.

Use the Internet to find out who's hiring, what their company does, who the key players are. It's merely one tool in your tool kit, not the toolbox itself. If you rely exclusively on the internet to find a job, you are likely in for a long, frustrating search.

Don't expect recruiters to bring a job to your door!

True Story! Really!

Simon received a generous severance package including career transition services. When he was asked if he wanted to start his services, he said, "I don't think I need to. I have several recruiters working for me."

Not so fast there, Simon.

Recruiters—they don't work for you. <u>Ever</u>. Read my ink. If you ever hear words resembling these come out of your mouth, or anyone else's for that matter, you will know that you (or they) are way off base: "I have a recruiter working for me." Nope. Follow the dollars. Who pays recruiters? You? Nope again.

In fact, it is not possible to pay someone to find you a job. Don't shell out the big bucks (or any bucks, for that matter) when someone tries to tell you otherwise. When someone loses their job, it is very common to start calling recruiters for help. It's not the wisest place to start, but many, many people do it. Ask any recruiter—they are bombarded by these calls. Most will genuinely try to help, but their ability to do so is limited. It is not in their interest as a business person to do so. Some of you may be thinking, "That's not true! They can make money by placing me!"

Let's back up. Recruiters get paid by clients (companies) who have specific positions that they are looking to fill. Their ability to "place" anyone is driven by whether that person matches any of the positions their clients have hired them to fill. If you are not a match, their ability to help you at all is minimal. In many cases, they won't even be interested in helping you.

Yes, it may be smart for recruiters to meet with everyone who asks to meet them. They do it on the chance that they might meet someone who will use *their* services when that person gets a job with a new company. And yes, maybe they should meet with everybody, just because it is always nice to help people.

But let's be realistic for a moment. Smart recruiters spend time on activities that make them money. A recruiter I know said that when he opened his firm, he resolved to call back every job seeker who contacted him. This is a guy who had been laid off himself, so he remembered what it's like to not get your call returned. He quickly discovered that it would be impossible to call everyone back, and still actually spend the time required to make his business successful. And he was just talking about returning calls, not actually taking meetings!

I've seen recruiters fall into one of two buckets—those who get the whole networking thing and those who don't. Some approach it tactically. They spend their time talking to, and meeting with, only those people who are possible fits for the jobs on their desk right then. If you don't fit, you may as well not exist—until they do get something that is a fit for you. Don't be offended. It's nothing personal.

The second type understands that building long term relationships is good for business. They are more likely to make time to meet with you, or at least give you some thoughts on your resume.

Keep in mind that you will always have more luck getting a meeting with a recruiter if you are referred by someone who already has a relationship with that recruiter.

Earlier, I told you the story of the recruiter who was inundated with 800 resumes? You were probably wondering how he thinned the herd. He started by singling out those who had the name of a referral source on their subject line. He figured it would be smart to start there, with the ones who had been referred by people he knew. Smart strategy, in my opinion. We are not as likely to allow people we don't think highly of to use our names. You know, that old guilt by association thing. When we receive a referral from someone, we at least should be able to assume that they are (probably) not a psycho killer. This recruiter used networking as a filtering strategy. Brilliant!

But why won't they return my calls? One of the biggest frustrations I hear voiced about recruiters is that they don't return calls. Go back and reread the previous few paragraphs if you still don't understand why that may be.

True Story! Really!

While she was employed, Norah received calls from recruiters a few times a month. Although she was happily employed at the time, she always took their calls. She figured even if she wasn't interested in what they had to say, maybe she could help a friend out. Besides, she knew that building relationships is easier before you need something—and this applies to recruiters as well. Good girl, Norah! When she lost her job, she picked up the phone and let all those recruiters she had helped know about her new situation. Predictably, they all returned her calls and were happy to keep her in mind. They even gave her some great contacts.

The best time to develop relationships with recruiters is when you don't need anything. (Actually, that is the best time to develop a relationship with anyone) When a recruiter calls you at your current job, looking for candidates for a position they have been hired to fill, take the time to talk to them. Even if you are knee-deep in alligators at work. Help them so that when you need something in the future (and you probably will), they remember you fondly. Give them names. Send them suggestions and ideas for their searches.

Those annoying recruiter calls you used to avoid? Maybe that's not such a good long-term career strategy after all, eh?

Another thing you need to know about recruiters is that they are hired to put a square peg in a square hole. Not a round peg, not an oval peg, not a peg that is round but really thinks it can be square, given a chance. This may annoy the heck out of you if you don't get clear on it.

Recruiters aren't interested in your desire to change careers, or your desire to be a rock star. They want square pegs—and as square as possible, please. That's why the client is paying them a not-so-small sum. So don't be disappointed when your pleas to be considered for a job that really isn't a fit for you fall on deaf ears, even though you know you'd be really awesome at it.

Recognize that hiring is about your ability to do the job, as well as your fit, or chemistry—whatever you want to call that intangible stuff. That "stuff" is also on the recruiter's mind. You may be ideal on paper, but your ability to fit in to the company culture, and mesh with the team, matters just as much. And it is the recruiter's job to assess that as well. She knows the company and the personalities involved. She will make that call.

Digging out of the Big, Black Hole: Following up, the right way

True Story! Really!

DeeDee came to a meeting of job seekers, optimistic about an interview she had, but perplexed as to why the HR person wasn't returning her calls. She had left two messages, but still hadn't heard back. She said, "I looked up the HR person's home address. I'm going to stop by her house on my way home." This story might push the bounds of your willingness to believe that I am actually telling you true stories. This is absolutely a true story.

Luckily, the group was able to stop her.

Searching for a job can make people crazy. The waiting, the wondering, the anticipation, the disappointment—sometimes all in the same ten minute period.

When you find a job you would really, really like to have, it's easy to get over-eager. You think you interviewed well. The interviewer talked about next steps. You ran home and sat by the phone, certain that the company was just adding extra zero's to your offer.

Then nothing happens. They said they'd make a decision about what they want to do next by Tuesday. Now it's Friday. You analyze everything you did, what you wore, and how you answered every question, just trying to figure out how you screwed it up.

Stop torturing yourself. In most cases, it is not you. Although your search is your number one priority, filling the open position is not all the company has on their plate. I have found that hiring managers are often overly optimistic about how long it takes to hire someone. They often don't think about letting you know that the time-frame has changed. But we personalize (and awfulize) the situation, which causes overreactions.

Remember, desperate and needy are not sought-after qualities in any organization.

If you are feeling desperate and needy, never pick up the phone until you are sure you can keep those feelings under wraps. If a hiring manager senses those feelings in you, it will come across and diminish your chances.

The how and when of follow-up

OK, so you have applied for a position, but you haven't heard anything yet. (I know, it's shocking, right?) How can you follow-up with the company without looking totally desperate, making the hiring manager think you're a stalker? Here are a few tips, depending on how you have applied:

1. If you have applied online.

If it is a blind ad, (meaning there is no company name attached to the ad) follow-up is not really possible.

If you know who the company is, and applying online is the method requested, then activate your network for contacts inside the company. Never stop with just an online application if at all possible. If you can find out who the hiring manager is, or who the HR person responsible for filling the job is, pick up the phone and call.

What do you say once you get someone from Human Resources on the line? When I was in HR, one of my pet peeves was getting a call that said, "I am just checking to see if you got my application." To me, that says, "Please stop whatever you are doing and look for my application among the hundreds you probably got."

I have found it to be much more effective to leave a very professional, upbeat message like, "This is Emma Clark. I applied for the position of IT Infrastructure Manager and wanted to reiterate my interest in the position. I believe that my last three years' experience in a similar role with the XYZ Company makes me well qualified. If you have any questions about my application, I can be reached at this number."

You have just positioned yourself as professional, pleasant, and proactive. In fact, the person who receives the message may just go look for your application. You are no longer words on a page—you are a voice. Your next goal is to become a real person, with a face-to-face meeting.

2. If you have interviewed (on the phone or in person), and have not heard anything back.

First of all, always ask at the end of an interview when you should expect to hear back, either with the company's decision, or with the next steps. This will give you a general idea of a time-frame so you can follow up appropriately. If the next step is expected to happen within two weeks, call a few days after the two weeks have passed. DO NOT call at noon on the 14th day!

Repeat after me: "I am not desperate, I am not a stalker."

When you do make the call, say something like this: "Hi. This is Jeff Johnston. I interviewed two weeks ago for the Marketing Director position. I remain very interested in the position. Is there anything else you need from me to move the process forward?" Believe me, it accomplishes the same thing as saying, "I'm just checking to see if you have made a decision." But it's a better way to make contact, because in the first example, it's about what you can do for them. The second example is about what they can do for you.

Don't panic. It always takes longer than you expect it to, even if they acted like you were exactly who they'd been searching for during the interview. The only antidote is to spend your time digging up new opportunities so that if this one goes south, you aren't stuck with an empty pipeline.

Remember to always stay professional, even if you don't get the job. You never know when things will change drastically, and an opportunity will open up because of your class and graciousness. I'll leave you with this story:

True Story! Really!

Haley had her eye on a position that she thought would be the perfect fit. Unfortunately, they had decided to bring back the top two candidates, and she was number three. Undeterred, she decided not to give them the last word. She wrote them a very gracious letter, thanking them for their time and interest, expressing how much she enjoyed meeting the team. She ended it by saying that she remained very interested in the organization, and hoped that they could find opportunities in the future to work together.

Two months later, she got a call from the hiring manager. The candidate they selected had accepted the job, then quit two weeks later for an even better opportunity. Would she still be available by any chance? The hiring manager later told Haley that her letter is what caused them to pick up the phone. Her professionalism and maturity, and her interest in taking a long-term view with the company, convinced them that they needed to give her a second look.

Final thoughts on staying out of the Big Black Hole

It's really easy to get sucked into that black hole of relying on the internet for the bulk of our job search activity. It's also easy to launch ourselves into that same black hole by making bad decisions about things like recruiters and follow-up.

The thing to remember is that even if you realize that you are in a big black hole, you can get out of it. (Unless of course you showed up at the HR director's house to "have a little talk." You probably won't get a job with that company. Plus, searching for a job is tough when you're in jail.) It's not too late to start doing the things the right way.

Bottom line? You can't depend on the internet, recruiters, or anyone else to find the right job for you. All these things can be great tools, but ultimately, you are in charge of finding that perfect job.

MISTAKE 5

SPENDING TOO MUCH TIME AT NETWORKING EVENTS (BUT NOT REALLY NETWORKING)

...AND I REMEMBER THE TIME,
AS A LITTLE GIRL, GOING
ON A CANOE TRIP...

BE THIS GUY...

Meredith carefully tracked her job search networking time—and her outcomes. She went to group meetings armed with goals: who she wanted to meet, and what she wanted to learn. If she was not able to meet her goals after attending a couple of a particular group's meetings, she reevaluated her future attendance. She left each meeting having set up a follow-up appointment with at least one potentially high-value contact.

...NOT THIS GUY

Peter was a fixture on the job seekers' networking circuit. You name an event, he was there. He was there early. He stayed late. He pressed the flesh relentlessly. When asked about his networking activity, he could proudly recite all of the groups in town he was involved in. In fact, he even took a leadership position with one. He was a group-aholic.

Don't misunderstand. I love networking groups for job seekers. But I do think you can effectively network and land a job without attending even one networking event. Your success as part of a networking group depends on your style and your preferences.

Before I go any farther in this chapter, I need to give you my definition of networking. I define it this way:

Networking is the building of mutually beneficial relationships that support your goals.

Right now, your goal is finding a job. But the "mutually beneficial" part must still be a part of your networking. When you are unemployed, you may feel like you have nothing to give.

True Story! Really!

Art looked grumpy. I had asked him to attend a networking meeting where I was speaking. I promised that I would introduce him around. As an introvert, this was uncomfortable territory for him.

Here we were at this event, and there he was—sitting all alone, looking mighty miserable. I gave him my best stern look and he jumped to his feet. I happened to be talking to someone who was in his field. A quick introduction, and they were off and chattering. Could he have found this contact himself? Of course. The problem was, he didn't know how.

For whatever reason, people shudder at the word "networking." I call it the ten-letter four-letter word. The word itself conjures up the visual of Joe Pocket-Full-of Business-Cards. You know this guy—he's the one that isn't letting anyone leave until they possess one of his cards, and have been the recipient of his smarmy charms. If that's the image you have of networking, then we need to reframe your perspective. Otherwise you have zero hope of using networking as a tool to land the job of your dreams.

More than 2/3 of people get their jobs through other people—people they already know, and new people they meet. When you realize that there are only four possible ways to get a job (direct mail, answering ads/postings, recruiters/agencies, and networking), you realize what a huge chunk that 2/3 actually is!

You will have two types of networking activities—attending groups and events, and one-on-one meetings. My experience is that you can find a job without ever attending a networking event, but it is much harder to find a job without ever having one-on-one meetings.

Making networking meetings more valuable—for you and everyone else!

If you decide to attend group meetings, here are some tips that will allow you make the most of the time you spend there:

- Go with a goal
- Wear your listening ears
- Look for opportunities to give something of value to the other people there
- Ask people about themselves
- Think of ways to be helpful
- Ask people about themselves (yes, I really did put this twice—it's that important!)

One of your goals should always be to find a reason to set up a one-on-one meeting with people from the meeting. (Even setting up a meeting with one person is enough!) Try to meet and get to know just a few people, instead of trying to dazzle every attendee with your charm.

One-on-one meetings: your most effective networking tool

The real power of networking is in the one-on-one meetings. It is in those meetings that we can begin to build mutually beneficial relationships. I'm not necessarily talking about lifelong best pals. I'm talking about professional contacts, and not all are created equal. You will have some networking meetings that go very well. You have a lot to talk about. You find many areas of common interest. Other meetings, well, don't go quite so smoothly. I call these the, "if I stick this fork in my eye, maybe I can leave early" meetings.

The conclusion you may be drawing is "I need to network, but I can stop once I find a job." Nope. Networking must be a career-long activity. Here's why. People are changing jobs at a faster pace than ever before. Let's say you find your next job through one of your newer networking contacts (we'll call her Josie), but two years into the job, the company is sold and you are in the market once again. "Ugh. I have to network again," you think.

You pick up the phone and call Josie. After all, she was so helpful last time! If this is the first time she has heard from you in two years, she is probably not going to want to help you again. And with good reason. At this point, you are a User. You only reach out when you need something. You don't like to be used, and neither do the people in your network.

True Story! Really!

Gary was a client of mine who landed a great job as a Chief Financial Officer. About a year after he started in this position, I had another client who I thought could benefit from some time with Gary. He was interested in the industry Gary was working in. I sent him two emails asking him if he would meet with this person. No response. I was puzzled, as Gary and I had a great relationship when we were working together.

I thought it must be some email glitch, so I picked up the phone and left him a message. No response. Of course, I was calling to ask for a favor, and his lack of response told me that he wasn't interested in granting one.

Fast forward two years. I get an email from Gary. I knew immediately that he had lost his job, and now he needed something. If he treated the rest of his contacts the way he treated me when he didn't need anything from me, my guess is that he didn't get much help on his new search.

Has this happened to you in this or some other areas of your life? Most of us have people we only hear from when they want something. Doesn't feel good, does it? Don't be a Gary.

Networking when you have an immediate need will always be less comfortable than networking when you don't. When you call people and ask to meet while you are unemployed, you know that they know why you are calling. They may respond like this: "I don't know of any jobs," or, "My company isn't hiring."

Warning: If you ever call someone and begin the conversation with, "I lost my job, know of any?" or, "I lost my job. You hiring?" I will track you down and beat you with the book you are now holding. No one carries a list of jobs in their back pocket. It's like saying on a first date "I think you're cute. I think we might get married. How 'bout it?" Anyone you approach like this will run for the hills—and they should!

The purpose of networking is to gather information about companies—what they are doing, and what their "pain" is. You tell your story, and find out of you are a possible fit, now or in the future.

How do you approach someone to set up a one-on-one networking meeting? Here is one possible scenario, starring Good Networker Kelly:

Kelly: "Hi Don, this is Kelly Browne. You may have heard that my company closed its doors last week. I am now looking for a new opportunity. I've heard good things about your company. I would love to have the opportunity to find out more about what you are doing, and see if my skills and experience might be a fit, now or in the future."

Don: "I am so sorry to hear that! That must be tough. I'd love to help, but we're not hiring right now."

Kelly: "OK, bye!"

(That was a trick…of course she doesn't say "OK, bye!" Duh! This is what she actually says:)

Kelly: "That's okay. I'm really just interested in learning more about what you guys are doing. I didn't expect that you would be hiring right now. Can I buy you a cup of coffee sometime next week?"

See why I call her Good Networker Kelly?

Your chances of actually getting an opportunity to chat with Don increase greatly once he sees that you are not expecting him to get you a job. Here's the way this scenario plays out, more often than you might think: Don has an opportunity to sit down with Kelly, without feeling like he has to have a list of jobs in his back pocket He begins to really understand who she is and what she has done. He is impressed by what he sees and hears.

He actually does know of an opportunity within his company, or at least someone else she should meet. And Kelly is off and running! I can think of several instances where clients went in for a chat with someone at a company, having been warned that they weren't hiring. By the end of the chat, the interviewer "all of a sudden" thought of a potential opportunity, and sends the interviewee off immediately to talk with a few others. Magically, hiring happens! Guess what? No other candidates ever got an opportunity to even be considered.

I believe that many people truly want to help you find work, but their ability to help may be limited. For instance, some people in your network may be great at lending emotional support on tough days. Others may be great at helping you strategize and think clearly about your options, while someone else may be very well connected in your field. The trick is to figure out what kind of help you want from each contact, and not being afraid to ask for it.

There is nothing worse than a networking meeting without purpose. Your contact feels like they can't help because you haven't asked for exactly what you need. The conversation meanders. Sure, it might fun to catch up, or learn about a new contact. But before you go in to any networking meeting, get very clear about what you are asking for so that your contact will understand how they can help you.

True Story! Really!

Mark really got the networking thing. He had probably networked with 200 people by the time he got connected with Joe, the head of a local Chamber of Commerce. As you might imagine, Joe networked regularly as a part of his job. He was a willing and able networking partner. He was also a very busy guy who liked to get straight to the point.

As soon as they sat down he asked, "What specifically can I help you with today?" Mark, with 200 networking meetings under his belt, was taken aback. No one had ever asked this question so directly. He left the meeting wondering how many times during those 200 meetings he had similarly "peed on his shoes."

Joe was right, wasn't he? Although few, if any, of the people you network with will actually ask the question, it's the one everyone has on their mind. "What can I help you with?" Having a networking meeting just for the sake of saying you had one is a waste of everyone's time. So don't set up a meeting until you are ready to have focused, meaningful conversations. With some of your contacts, you will only get one opportunity to impress them. Don't blow it by wasting their time.

How much networking should you do? The quick answer is, as much as you can do, and still maintain your energy. Networking is especially hard for introverts, as it depletes their energy. So they should plan to have fewer networking meetings, but be focused on getting the most out of each one they do.

One of the key skills a person needs in order to network effectively is the ability to listen. This works in the favor of introverts, because introverts are typically good listeners. (Extroverts? They are waiting for you to shut up so they can talk again!)

You can't find out what your networking partner needs, or how you may be able to "give," without listening, can you?

Some final thoughts on networking

As I said before, most people who are working today owe their jobs to the fact that they knew someone who helped them get that job. People like to help other people. When you network, you give people a chance to help you. And you get the chance to help people in return.

I can't think of a better investment of your time and energy!

MISTAKE #6

CASTING YOUR NET TOO WIDELY

(THE IMPORTANCE OF A TARGET LIST AND A NETWORKING STRATEGY)

BE THIS GUY...

Jenna was very clear on what her skills were. She spent some real time figuring out what organizations would be the best fit for her, from a cultural perspective, and a job responsibilities perspective. She had a target list of companies she was interested in and a list of people she wanted to meet.

...NOT THIS GUY

Charles wanted a job. He decided to employ the "throw it against the wall to see what would stick" strategy. He figured that if he sent out thousands of resumes, surely something would hit. He even signed up for one of those services that promise to send your resume all over Planet Earth, and beyond. Action = productivity, he thought. When someone asked him what he wanted to do, he stayed intentionally vague. Why close down opportunities, right?

Seems counterintuitive, I know. When you want a job, when every fiber of your being and every hour in your day are seemingly spent on that goal, you want to give yourself as many options as possible. Tell the world! Surely someone will see your value, and truck sacks of cash to your front door.

You blast your resume everywhere, to everyone you can think of. You attend every networking meeting in town. You are getting nowhere. You are exhausted.

I hear this way too often. There is a real fear of getting specific, of missing an opportunity to do X because you said you wanted to do Y.

It is very important that your search be focused. Go back and reread that until you hear it, and commit it to memory.

Companies are not seeking people who are "really open to whatever you have available." Let's take a walk to the company side of the hiring desk. If you have ever been in the position to hire, you know what a tough process it can be. You know how important it is to find exactly the right person—the person who is going to make your pain go away, and who will hit the ground running.

You want to find the person who is excited about the exact job you are offering, who believes this job is a perfect fit. You are most certainly not seeking someone who is just looking for a job, someone who says things like, "I have a lot of transferable skills and can do a lot of things. I'm really not set on any one type of job. I'm a quick learner and love working with people." Snore.

no

That person is probably not a good hire. They do not know what they are looking for. They have not done the hard work of self-analysis, then moved to the next step, which is to ask themselves, "Where do I want to work?" "What will make me wildly happy?" "What kind of company culture is best for me?"

No one is a fit for all jobs, or for all companies. The sooner you figure out where you should cast your net, the more successful you will be.

True Story! Really!

Isabella was a strategic, thoughtful, people-focused HR leader. The bulk of her career had been spent working for a company whose values aligned with her own. The employees were treated like real people. Their policies and programs showed that they lived out their values.

Her world changed when the company was purchased by another, much larger organization whose HR philosophy was directly the opposite of hers. She had the opportunity to stay with them, but declined. Unfortunately, her next two jobs were with organizations whose people philosophies were equally draconian.

She finally ended up starting her own HR consulting firm, where she could set the tone and develop the culture. Looking in her own rear view mirror, she realized that although the money was great in her last couple of assignments, she had failed to recognize the importance of aligning her core values with those of her employer. "I was spoiled," she said, "I thought every company would be like my first, so I failed to spot culture as a must-have. If I had, with careful networking, I could have discovered that each of those opportunities were wrong for me." And I would have conducted a more effective search by really developing the target list that reflected me.

Importance of Target Lists

A target list is a list of organizations (typically 30-50) that seem to be aligned with your values, your skills, your interests and offer the kind of work that you want to do. It's based on the research you have done on the company, including the company culture. They are the organizations that you are the most interested in right now. If you are working with an outplacement firm, they will tell you how important it is to develop a target list.

If you are like most people, you will nod in agreement, and promptly ignore that advice.

Resist the urge to ignore. In my experience, a target list is one of the most critical tools in your job search tool kit. I can hear all of your objections now, because I have heard them all before. Let's start knocking them down.

How am I supposed to develop such a list?

Your list will come from multiple sources: chamber of commerce sites, your local business journal and other newspapers, databases available through your local library, from your networking contacts, and from your own personal experience. You should also tap into the input and experience of others. Look at company websites, read about what they are involved in, talk to your network, talk to people that work at these companies now, or did in the past.

Can I just make a list of the 50 largest companies in my geography?

No. Any monkey can do that. Don't tell me that every one of those 50 companies is a great fit for you. I have seen people do that, and what that says to me is that you were too lazy to give it any thought. I know you haven't really been trying when I see the most conservative, rigid company in town (the one where you dare not leave your desk without wearing your suit coat) on the same list with the most freewheeling, edgy company in town (the one where people take their dogs to work).

You will not be equally happy at both, and don't try to convince anyone that you will be.

But Julie, my skills are entirely transferable! I can work anywhere!
Won't a target list limit my opportunity?

Absolutely not! In fact, I believe that it increases your odds of landing the right job (remember, that is the goal!) because you are prepared, focused, and thoughtful. These are very attractive qualities to a hiring manager. But, you do have to spend real time and thought on preparing your list, because you must be ready when you are asked why certain companies are on that list.

Imagine that you are in a networking conversation. You are explaining to your networking partner that ideally, you would like to work for a mid-sized company in the consumer packaged goods industry or a large marketing services firm. You see him thinking about how to help you, trying to think of companies that meet your criteria.

Now imagine the power of whipping out a list of the companies in your geography that meet your criteria. I promise you that you have just increased the likelihood of that person being able to be helpful by tenfold. I have seen it many, many times. He pulls out his pen and starts making notes, giving you information, ideas, and contacts. You have just helped him help you. You have focused his thinking. You will also spark ideas about other companies that aren't on your list.

If there is a company I have forgotten to put on my list, (or maybe I didn't even know about it!) won't people think I am not interested in that company?

Again, no. Remember, this list is a "living" list, not one cast in stone. Companies will hop on and off the list, based on what you learn about them in the course of your networking. The very existence of this list will ignite great conversations with your networking partners.

True Story! Really!

Thad was a senior level guy with broad experience. Try as I might, I could not convince him to create a target list. Creating a target list requires that you have clarity about what you want to do—and where you want to do it. We went around and around on it. He would never put a stake in the ground and express a preference of what he wanted to do, or where he might want to do it. He became frustrated with me because I wouldn't give him names from my network. But how could I know which ones to give him? All of them? I think not.

Importance of Networking Lists &
a Networking Strategy

You already know that you are most likely to get your next job through someone you know or someone you meet—through good, old-fashioned networking. You probably also know that all relationships are not created equal. There are people you are closer to than others. That means you have "permission" to ask for different things, based on your relationship. I use three very simple categories to define how close a person's relationship is with someone else: A's, B's and C's. Put everyone you know in one of those categories as follows:

A's. These are people who know you well, either personally or professionally. They think highly of you. They are in a position to help, and most likely, they are very willing to help. They will not only take your calls and make time for you, but will meet with you more than once. They may even call you once they hear that you are on the market.

B's. These are people who you know. But either you don't know them as well, or you are not quite sure of their interest or ability to help. They will take your calls and will most likely meet with you. But you may only get one chance to meet with them. You really want to be crisp, polished and focused during that meeting.

C's. This group includes people you would like to meet, or you know peripherally, but maybe not well enough to get to on your own. They would most likely take your call, and you may be able to convince them to meet with you.

You should always start networking with your A's first because their interest in your search is usually higher. They are most likely to be invested in your success. These folks can speak more credibly to your many skills and charms. They are likely go out on more limbs on your behalf because they are certain that you will make them look good. And we all like to look good!

They will also be more likely to tell you when your messages are unclear or when you are off track in your search. You can't have too many of those honest people who care around you.

> ### *True Story! Really!*
>
> Annie came to see me in tears. Her sister was president of a local professional association and, as a result, was quite well networked. Fortuitously for Annie, her sister's network was made up of all of the people that Annie wanted to meet. What luck! Jobs should drop from the sky! Unfortunately, Annie's sister didn't get the "networking thing," and was not helpful at all. Try as she might, Annie could not get her sister to make one introduction on her behalf.

Know this. As sure as the sun will set tonight, some of your A's will disappoint you, and some of your C's will pleasantly surprise you. Try not to take it too personally. Not everyone knows how to help. Some won't really understand what you need, and some will just plain not want to help. Just promise me that you will never be that person.

Make sure your meetings have a purpose!

Very important! You must always have a reason to meet with someone. More specifically, ask yourself this question: WHY would that person want to meet with you? Because you asked? That will work with your A's, if they are truly A's. Everyone else may need to understand exactly what you want to accomplish before they make time in their undoubtedly busy schedules. Each of your contacts will be able to help in different ways. Let them know in advance what you are asking of them.

Ways networking contacts can be helpful

- Giving you feedback on your resume.

- Giving you feedback on your skills and areas of strength.

- Sharing information about the geographic market you are targeting.

- Giving you information about companies on your target list.

- Introducing you to key people in their network.

- Connecting you to opportunities they hear about.

- Commiserating with you on bad days and celebrating with you on good days.

Can you see how not everyone on your list can help you with every one of those items? For example, please do not expect your B's or C's (or even all of your A's) to commiserate with you! Be mindful of what you are asking people for. Remember that this job search is your top priority, but not the top priority of everyone else.

True Story! Really!

Edie was getting frustrated that John, one of her B networking contacts, had not yet called her back. She had left two messages. She was attending an event over the weekend and looked across the room and saw, you guessed it, John. He saw her and walked up to her and said, "Edie! How are you?" She said, in a tone of obvious irritation, "Growing old waiting for you to call me back." As you might expect, John stammered and apologized.

Edie told me this story on the Monday after the event, very proud of herself for letting John know exactly how she felt. John knew he had yet to return her call, and after seeing her in person, he likely would have mentioned his lack of response. He may have even set up a time to talk right then and there. Making someone feel bad is not the way to get favors.

Final thoughts on targeting your job search

Have you ever seen a dog, chasing a whole flock of birds? They usually end up not catching any of them, because they end up turning around in every different direction. If they just went after one bird, they might have a chance.

The same thing is true of your job search. If you try to go in too many directions, you won't catch anything. The smart way to search is the way I described in this chapter: target the companies you think will be a good fit for you. Then use your networking contacts in a strategic way to find out which companies might have an opening.

When you focus your energy on the best companies for you, and the people who can help you the most, you greatly increase your chances of finding the right job for you.

And isn't this all about you finding the right job?

MISTAKE #7

OVERLOOKING THE "GIMME" QUESTIONS
(...AND OTHER INTERVIEWING UH-OHS)

YOU CAN'T ASK ME
THAT... IT'S AGAINST MY
CONSTITUTIONAL RIGHTS.

BE THIS GUY...

Camille was a highly capable professional who knew her many talents and believed that she would, and should, have many options. She was contacted by the hiring manager at one of her target companies and asked to come in and interview. She asked for a job description in advance, and for the names and titles of all of the people she would be meeting with. She found out what she could about the company and the interviewers through her many sources. She got ready for the interview by matching up her qualifications with what the position description said they were looking for. She prepared work examples that highlighted her skills in action.

...NOT THIS GUY

Todd had an interview. The hiring manager said, "Just come on in Todd. We want to get to know you." "How hard could that be?" thought Todd. "They can't stump me, because who knows me better than me?" Besides, this was just a "get to know ya" session. No preparation necessary then, eh?

Ah yes, the interview. Gawd, don't you hate being interrogated, I mean, interviewed.

Don't be such a sissy! Think of it this way. An interview is a conversation between two or more professionals aimed at determining whether YOU WILL BE DEEMED GOOD ENOUGH TO WORK THERE, OR IF YOU WILL LIVE THE REST OF YOUR LIFE IN A CARDBOARD BOX JUST OFF THE CLOSEST EXIT RAMP.

Okay, come on down off the ledge. It's not that bad.

Hiring is about pain. Always. No pain, no reason to hire.

Let's break it down. **Companies hire people because they have a need or needs that are going unmet.** Go back and read that again. If they do not have a need, they will not hire you or anyone else. Nothing you can do will change that, regardless of how desperately you want a job at that company!

Once the decision has been made that yes, needs are going unmet, and pain is indeed being experienced, the big question in the mind of an employer is, "Are you the one that is best equipped to make our pain go away?" Ah. A complex question indeed.

Being your best in interviews

Since each interviewer is different, there is no way to know for sure what you are going to face when you walk into an interview situation. But some things seem to come up over and over again with people I have worked with. So here are a few things you are likely to face in the interview process:

Not finding even one skilled, competent, unbiased
interviewer during your search.

Hiring decisions are made by people, who as we know, are quite complex in their thought processes, judgment, and decision-making ability. Plus, they are chock full o' biases. ("Hmmm…he looks just like that guy we hired two years ago who was a bust/my uncle who was a creep/the guy who dumped me. Let's pass.")

Don't laugh. I really think that is as logical as some people's hiring thought process gets. Why? Because they have no clue HOW to make a good hiring decision. That's why some companies become overly reliant on assessment tools. They are seeking some sort of sure-fire way to make a good decision. If you can figure out how to make sure that happens, you can start shopping for your own island.

Hiring decisions are highly subjective and are often driven by gut instinct. Companies spend a lot of money developing hiring processes and systems to try to eliminate the bias. You may have experienced behavioral interviewing. It's the one where you are asked for specific examples of things that you've done. (More on that later in this chapter.)

I am a big fan of this process. I have taught it to people on both sides of the hiring desk. It does mean a need for copious amounts of preparation, not to mention anti-perspirant, as it can be quite stressful.

At one point in my career, I taught this method to a group of managers. I found that some managers were quite receptive to improving their skills, and very much welcomed the training. Others, however, were quite content with the way they'd always done it, which typically included illegal or highly inappropriate questions.

Back in the day, managers had become very comfortable asking questions that could and did get both them and their companies in trouble. Most just played the odds that they wouldn't get caught, and kept doing it their way.

Yes, you will undoubtedly meet some of these people in your interviewing journey. You'll recognize them by the way they dismissively toss the prepared and approved interview guide aside, and say some version of, "Why don't we just get to know each other?" Watch out! This is often followed by a question about marital status, children, or the church you attend.

Interviewers who think they can make good decisions through the answers to these questions are scary—and yes, they do still exist. The question you need to ask yourself is, "Do I want to work for someone like this?"

I think I have seen it all, but I probably haven't. In the Introduction, I mentioned a client whose interviewer fell asleep in the middle of the interview. I have to say, that floored me. I'm not exactly sure what the right thing to do is in a case like that. (Unless it would be waiting until he wakes up, and enthusiastically accepting the overly generous offer that you pretend he made while sleeping.) While I've never heard of this happening before, or since, I have been a part of many interviews where a quick nap would have been preferable to—and more productive than—the interview itself.

Ignoring warning signs during the selection process.

First of all, let's get this perfectly clear: it matters how a company treats you in the interview process. It is a clear indicator of how you will be treated as an employee. Do I have scientific data to back this up? No. But think of it this way. Both parties should be putting their best foot forward, because everyone is sizing each other up in order to make the best decision possible.

So why is it that employers often act as if they have the cookie and you are the hungry little boy? The more you jump for it, the farther they hold it away. There is all too often an attitude that "we have what you want," and given that, they don't have to try very hard. (Part of it may be because you act like a hungry little boy—desperate for a cookie, any cookie.)

Of course, not all employers are like that. Some truly understand that in order to attract the best talent available, they have to work hard and smart to find, land and retain the best people. Maybe it is just my jaded view, but those employers seem to be the exception.

If you've been in a search before, I am betting that you agree with that assessment.

This is like dating. If they don't treat you well during the "courtship," why on earth would you think it is going to be any better after you say "I do?"

Thinking all cookies will or should taste equally good to you!

Joe, a former colleague of mine, used to say that job satisfaction is pretty easy to find. It's just doing what you like, and what you're good at, in a place and with people that you like. Of course, he said that tongue-in-cheek, as we all know that true job satisfaction is a very complex formula that differs for each of us. Plus it changes over time as the rest of your life changes. The interview is simply one way to figure out how close you are to finding satisfaction.

Even though we psych ourselves out to the contrary, interviewing is a two-way street, and must be approached that way. The company is trying to decide if you are the best candidate for the job, and you are trying to decide EXACTLY THE SAME THING. You will not be a fit for every job, nor should you strive to be. If the hole is square, pretending to be square (even though you are as round as a button) is a surefire recipe for your own personal disaster.

I believe there are hundreds of thousands, if not millions, of round people who walk out of the door each morning, pretend to be square all day at work, then try to morph back to their natural roundness when the work day ends. Sound familiar? It wears me out just thinking about it.

You should interview as many times as you can in your quest for the right job. Yes, rejection is a part of the process. You will reject certain jobs, and you will be rejected.

Because being unemployed can be an emotionally precarious state, it feels really yucky to get a "no." Yes, sometimes it is you. More often than you might imagine, the "no" or the silence from an employer you interviewed with is NOT about you.

Positions are put on hold, cancelled, changed, rethought, revisited, or back-burnered for a large variety of reasons. Yes, it is extremely frustrating, and yes, it seems to be personal, because after all, it is happening to you. To compound the frustration, companies often go silent, figuring that you'll get the hint and go away. Ugh. There you are, thinking it is something that you've done or not done, the color of your tie, or the way you answered that 4th question.

But yes, sometimes you are just not a fit. That is their call—just like it is your call to say no to a company's request to interview you a second time. Get used to the fact that you may never know why a second interview is not forthcoming.

It is not in a company's interest to tell you that you seemed inflexible, or your style seemed too heavy handed for their culture. What's in it for them to tell you? All you'll do is try to tell them why they're wrong, and that you really are quite flexible, or that you are really just a big ol' teddy bear. Doesn't matter. They have made their decision, and you need to move on.

Forgetting that every conversation you have is some type of interview.

I was once asked to speak at an event about the topic of "talking to decision makers." It was holiday time, and the leader of the event was thinking about all of the parties these job seekers would be attending. What if, while hovering over the cheese tray, you encountered the woman who is the hiring manager at your ideal company? What do you say, "Swiss or gouda?" As I prepared for that presentation, I realized that we are all decision makers. It's just that the decisions we are in a position to make are very different. The hiring manager has a hiring decision to make. It will be either yes, no, or maybe.

The hiring manager's sister, who also happens to be your neighbor, has a very different decision to make. But it might be just as important for you. She's wondering if she should introduce you to her sister, the hiring manager.

Pretty important decision, wouldn't you say? Yet we tend to forget that getting to the ultimate decision maker isn't always a straight path. We usually have to go through several other layers to get there. Remember that it's a small world, and you never know who's watching you. Behave.

Not realizing that a "no" just might be a "not right now."

Will interviewed for a role that he thought was a good fit. In addition, he really liked the company and the people he interviewed with. He could see himself being very happy there. Imagine his disappointment when he got that "no thanks" letter. What does Will do now?

A. Lay on the couch and watch the Judge Judy Marathon.

B. Prank call the company until the receptionist is in tears.

C. Craft a "big boy letter."

I am hoping that you recognize the folly of anything resembling A and B. What's a "big boy letter?" I'm glad you asked!

When a company has to say no to a reasonably good candidate, they don't enjoy saying no any more than you enjoy hearing it—especially if you came in second or third. It's just something they have to do, because there is typically only one job to be filled.

When we get a no, it is typical to cross that company off our list. If you were lukewarm on the company in the first place, go ahead and cross it off. But if it was one, like Will, you were really excited about, don't give up. There are levels of "not giving up," so it's important to recognize the difference between appropriately staying in touch and a restraining order with your name at the top.

If you really want to stay on a company's radar screen, when you get that rejection letter, don't let them have the last word. Send a letter back, thanking them for their time, and telling them that you enjoyed learning about the company and meeting their team. Tell them that you would be very interested in being considered for future opportunities. In other words, you are saying, "I'm a big boy, I can take bad news."

This creates "permission" for the company to cross over the bridge again if there is another opportunity to consider you. They don't have to wonder whether you are still interested, or upset at your previous rejection. I have seen this work like a charm many times. Clients have been contacted for future positions.

However, if they determined that you were not a fit for the company, rather than not the best fit for that particular position, that won't work.

Send your letter to the person or people that you had the best chemistry with, who seemed to be your fans.

Failing to prepare in an effective way.

You know you have to prepare. You go to the library and check out all the books you can find on interviewing:

- The 500 Questions you Must Know How to Answer

- The 10,001 Ways to Prepare for your Interview

- Three Zillion Interview Questions that Can Kill Your Career Forever—and Leave You Destitute

Okay, I made all of those up, but you know there are books similar to those on your desk right now.

The essence of interview preparation comes down to this: being ready to pull examples and stories out of your experience that match up with what the company is seeking. How on earth can you know what the company is seeking, you ask?

Start with job postings, job descriptions, research on the company and the interviewers, both online and in talking to your contacts. The internet is a great tool for finding out about your interviewers, and hopefully finding something in common with one or more of them.

Maybe you and one interviewer have both worked at the same employer in the past. Perhaps you went to the same college as another interviewer. All of these are things to talk about and connect on.

Think about your qualifications. What in your experience, education, knowledge, and skills qualify you for this job? Put two columns on a piece of paper. On the left side of the paper, make a list of what the employer is seeking, or appears to be seeking. On the right side, write down what you have to offer that is a match for the items on the left.

Get ready to tell stories or give examples of times that you have used your key skills to accomplish something. This is behavioral interviewing. Sit in front of the mirror, or with an honest friend and practice telling those stories. Trust me, it sounds very different coming out of your mouth than it does between your ears.

DO NOT make a list of those 500 questions and memorize an answer to each. If the interviewer fails to ask you a question on your list, you may freeze up. Remember, interviewers are people, and people are unpredictable. I doubt if your interviewers have read that same book in preparation for interviewing you.

Todd (from the beginning of this chapter) is right in one respect. No one knows you better than you, so get very clear on what you bring to the table. Be ready to tell stories that illustrate you at your best.

Being interviewed is like anything else in life: you will get better at it the more you do it. I know that there are other skills in your life that you'd rather develop, but for this point in your life, this is an essential skill to master.

Thinking that the interviewer will see your brilliance on his own.

I'm sure you're a superstar like no other. Lesser mortals quake in your presence. Organizations will be lining up at your door any minute to shower you with embarrassingly large buckets o' cash. Uh Huh.

When you were with your previous organization, you may have interviewed internally for opportunities. If you're like most, you didn't prepare for that as rigorously as you would have for an external interview. Internally, your reputation precedes you, for better or for worse. Even in the largest organizations, the grapevine buzzes.

Internally, the interview still matters, but if you are thought to be difficult to work with or someone who talks a good game but doesn't deliver, it is hard to overcome that with a great interview. Likewise, if you are known to be someone who drives large and complex projects to outstanding results, working effectively with even the most difficult people, a so-so interview may not matter.

BUT…when it comes to interviewing with people who know nothing about you other than what you are going to tell them, the short period of time that you spend together matters in a big way. Do not expect the interviewers to read your mind, recognize your excellence, or hire you just because you smell good. Charm is overrated when it comes to hiring outstanding new team members.

Ignoring the gimme questions.

There are certain questions that you can almost bet you will be asked. So a big shame on you if you're not prepared.

Of course, as we discussed earlier in the book, Tell Me About Yourself is one of them. TMAY will be asked while you are networking and during an official interview.

Yes, it is hard to answer well. It is the ultimate open-ended question. Realistically, you could probably talk for days on this one. ("Do you want me to leave out the trauma I suffered on the kindergarten playground at the hands of that bully, Little Timmy Jones?") I believe this question gets asked for a number of reasons:

A. The interviewer is lazy/busy, and hasn't spent one minute looking at your resume. Now he's buying time by asking the question, hoping you will ramble so he can catch up.

B. The interviewer is unskilled, and has no clue what to ask.

C. She knows she is asking a very open ended question and wants to see what you choose to highlight. This can be great insight in to what you believe to be important about yourself.

D. He could be like an old manager of mine who said that because he knows the unprepared interviewee can go on forever. He asked it to see if the interviewee can actually answer it and shut up. He thought it was a way to measure one's "Results Focus."

It really doesn't matter why it gets asked. You'd better be prepared to answer it. If it is to be asked, it will be asked first. You can either put your interview on the right track or, all together now, "pee on your shoes". If you blow the first question out of the gate, it can be hard to recover.

(Helpful Hint: you are blowing this question when, 10 minutes into your answer, your interviewer's eyes have rolled completely back into his head, and you have to ask, "What was the question again?")

What are your Strengths?

I like this question.

What are your Weaknesses?

This one is not so great.

It doesn't matter what I think, though. Both will be asked, and both must be answered. I am hoping to hear an interviewing story some day that goes like this:

Interviewer: What are your weaknesses?

Interviewee: I'll take a pass on that one. Next question.

Okay, back to strengths. This is your opportunity to shine. Don't know your strengths? Thump yourself on the head for me.

You should have three key strengths selected and thought through ahead of time. You should also have two examples/stories of you in action, using each one. If you can't think of two high quality stories/examples, then they really aren't strengths, are they? Script these out in advance and be ready to draw the picture in words. If you don't, it could go something like this:

Skilled Interviewer: "What are your three key strengths?"

Goofy Interviewee: "I am very strong when it comes to solving complex problems, especially those that require working cross-functionally. In addition, I am very analytical. I am skilled at taking large amounts of data, then developing strategic plans based on that data. Finally, I am considered an expert in the use of social media in developing business."

Skilled Interviewer: "Can you give me an example of a time when you have used each strength?"

Goofy Interviewee: "Uh, no."

Okay, I know that you really wouldn't do that. You'd probably come up with something and stumble through it. That's not so impressive, especially when the topic is your strengths—something that you should be very familiar with, and highly conversant in.

Now, let's talk weaknesses. As I said, it's a bad question. It's one that everyone is prepared for, but generally prepared for in an inauthentic way. Does this scenario sound familiar?

Gullible Interviewer: "What are your weaknesses?"

Interviewee: "I just work so hard! I hold myself to such high standards!"

Gullible Interviewer: "Coincidentally, we are looking for people with high standards! Oh, happy day!"

Blah, blah, blah.

I always want to roll my eyes when I hear that kind of response. It's the "take a strength and call it a weakness and hope the interviewer is too dumb to notice" approach. Sadly, some people get away with it. Here's how a skilled interviewer would handle that answer:

Skilled Interviewer: "What are your weaknesses?"

Goofy Interviewee: "I just work so hard! I hold myself to such high standards!"

Skilled Interviewer: "Tell me about a time when your "high standards" caused you a problem at work."

Goofy Interviewee: Gulp.

It is true that "too high" standards can cause problems, so if this is a sincere answer, examples can and should be forthcoming. But usually, it is an over-coached interviewee who is trying to get past giving a real answer.

So what is a good answer? First of all, this question can come in many forms, such as:

- What would your former managers say are the areas that you most need improvement in?

- What did your last performance appraisal say were your areas of opportunity for development?
- How have you improved yourself, based on feedback from others?

See? They are trying to trick you into answering the weakness question straight up. They are sick to death of hearing about your supernaturally "high standards!"

So what to do? Well, first of all, I believe that weaknesses are relative. If your goal is to be starting Center for the Chicago Bulls, I'm guessing you have many weaknesses RELATED TO THAT POSITION. But if the job you are seeking is somewhat related to the last job you had, that is a different answer altogether.

Be clear on what the requirements of the job are. Then do an honest assessment of what you have to learn, sharpen up, etc., to really do a great job.

Your weaknesses should:

- *Be "fixable."* Hint: if you're not that bright, no amount of seminar attendance is going to fix that. Presentation skills, computer skills, knowledge of a software package, knowledge of a product or industry are good examples of skills/areas that you can readily improve on.
- *Be something that you have already made progress on.* In other words, you recognized it earlier in your career, and have already made progress. You have an "improvement" story to tell. It is not that impressive to have a fixable, acknowledged weakness and have done nothing about it.

Your weakness should NOT:

- *Be something that is core to the job you are interviewing for.* For example, if your attention to detail is not strong, for heaven's sake, do not take a job where precision is core to doing the job well! If you find yourself in an interviewing situation like that, you are clearly barking up the wrong tree.

Why do you think you are a good fit for this role? aka, why should we hire you?

That's the whole reason you got all prettied up and went to the interview, isn't it? If you can't answer that, stay home next time.

Helpful Hint: "I'm a really, really hard worker who just loves people! I know I can do a great job," is not going to get it done. Everyone says that.

In many cases, this is asked toward the end of the interview. If you have a good idea if you are a fit, then you are better prepared to match your qualifications with the position requirements.

Pay attention to who you are interviewing with.

Are you talking to the Chief Financial Officer? Dazzle her with stories about how effectively you managed your P&L, not how you consider budgets "annoying."

What about the Manager of Human Resources? Prepare some stories that show you managing people situations effectively. Leave out the knee-slapper about how your entire staff is terrified of you.

Thank you notes.

Think of something that you talked about that you can reference in the note, something that shows that you paid attention. Or, if there is something that you want to reemphasize, or that you forgot to mention, the thank you note can be used to close that loop as well.

Email is also good, especially if time is of the essence. But if the person you are sending it to happened to mention that he doesn't use a computer, go back to ye olde business letter.

Final thoughts on interviewing

It's really easy to get discouraged during the interview process. One reason is because there are a lot of things that can go wrong during the process. Many of those things are completely out of your control. You are likely to run into employers who are going to put you through any of these things:

- Not return your calls
- Ignore your resume and application
- Go silent after you've been in for an all day interview
- Change their minds about what they want for the role—after they've interviewed you
- Freeze & unfreeze open jobs, seemingly at random
- Post jobs that they will most assuredly fill internally

What can you do about these things? Nothing. Zero. Zilch. Just like there are flaky, unpredictable workers, there are companies that operate the same way. It's part of the job search. A bad part, but a part nonetheless. But, to be honest, wouldn't you like to know about how a company operates before you start to work there? It's better to find out now.

Truth is, there are a ton of great companies out there, and some of them will be a fit for your experiences, skills, and values. Your best chance to find work at one of these great companies is to prepare yourself to have an interview that rocks! Leave 'em saying "We don't deserve someone that fabulous! But let's throw sacks of cash at her and hope she graces us with a "yes!"

And Finally....

So there you have it. Seven mistakes you may be making. My guess is that you are probably making more than one. However, it is hard to see ourselves objectively or rationally, especially while we are going through a difficult time. The best gift you can give yourself is a brutally honest self assessment AND the development of a network of people who will give you the truth as well. (And please don't bite their heads off when they tell you need to change your hair, or sharpen up your messages!)

I don't know you, but am willing to bet that there is something that you are great at. Maybe you did it in a previous job, or in a volunteer activity- those perfect moments when you are in your own zone, when no one else can do whatever you are doing as well as you can. Maybe it was just a fleeting moment, but I am certain that it exists somewhere in your past.

I wish for you the courage to find it, and then to find work or a whole career in which you can do that most of the time. Once you've had a job where you are your true self all day long, you will do anything to have it again.

And remember, there is a time, a place, a situation, a role in which you can honestly say…

YES, YOU WILL GET A JOB...BUT THEN WHAT?

Even if you land your Perfect 10 Job, it is critical that you do NOT sit back and take your eye off the career "ball." And yes, you will most likely be in the job market again (and again) before you take a seat in that big ol' retirement rocking chair. *(...and just between you and me, don't ever give 100% of yourself to your new employer. Keep some of your energy and time to devote to looking out for yourself and your career. If you don't, who will?)*

To help you keep your career front and center, I send out a career tip every week that I call my **Career Aha! of the Week.** You can sign up at www.congruitycareer.com or www.jobsearchscrewups.com

Wishing you the job (and career) you dream of!

Julie

P.S. As you know, this book is filled with client stories. I'd love to hear yours!

14 - ① departure statement
② what should we know about you
 (TMAY)
③ what kind of job are you
 looking for ?

! Do pg. 28, 29, 31, 34-36

66 phone msg, follow up

! p 75 - be excited, specific

91 - ltr when didn't get job
93 - what qualifies you
96 - 3 strengths
97-98 weaknesses
99 - thank you

8656353R0

Made in the USA
Lexington, KY
19 February 2011